Samuel Elbert Miner

Creation

The Power Behind Evolution

Samuel Elbert Miner

Creation
The Power Behind Evolution

ISBN/EAN: 9783337779139

Printed in Europe, USA, Canada, Australia, Japan

Cover: Foto ©Lupo / pixelio.de

More available books at **www.hansebooks.com**

CREATION;

— OR, THE —

Power Behind Evolution.

DISCLOSING

The Unity of Matter and Force.

S. E. MINER.

BURLINGTON, IOWA:
BURDETTE COMPANY.
1887.

COPYRIGHT,
1887.
WM. A. MINER.

TO THE READER.

THE book that is herewith placed in your hands "was not made but grew." It has come into its place as an unexpected visitant, to author as well as to reader, and the only apology for its appearance is that it could not be kept back because of an impulse in the mind of the author urging to self-assertion.

The voice of truth coming to his own mind with unlooked for messages, and guiding his mind in new paths of thought, said "Write," and he has written. At first a single lecture was prepared, but this only served to make others necessary, and so the body of the work was written. This will account for the peculiar style of composition, for some repetitions of thoughts and of quotations from authors. As he pressed lines of thought into unexplored fields it seemed necessary that he should reach ultimates of thought by several different paths—that he should strive to make his positions fully understood by giving "line upon line, precept upon precept, here a little and there a little." Great care has been taken to allow advanced thinkers and experimenters in science to give expression to their latest discoveries, and it was desired that no important facts should be excluded from the list of experimental truths. It has become necessary, in presenting this hypothesis of imponderable forces, for the author to differ from the teachings of some of our masters in science, and he trusts that an apology for so doing will be found in the self-asserting nature of the guiding principles to which he has committed himself as beacon lights in the unseen realms of mental discoveries. He has been compelled to press his thoughts of creation along new paths of guidance and has gained new conceptions of those imponderable forces that physicists have hitherto failed to classify as having a place among the states of matter. He has found space to have a significance in the domain of matter, and in its relation to the creative potencies that command it in all of its lines of motion, that seems never to have been thought worthy of notice in our schools of philosophy, and that exalts it to the place of a commanding sovereignty over matter and the first things of a material creation.

Where teachers failed to lead material forces have been accepted as guides, and where they have led the writer has ventured to follow. The domain of the forces is a new world for scientific discovery. In this new world there are sublime revelations of vast wonders, but no miracles. Sun-systems of worlds in the domain of space reveal themselves as units of creation in the embrace of material forces, submitting to quantitive measurements, and with possibilities reaching to the infinites of power and compassing the unmeasurable of space. In the field of the forces an invisible atom, a line of force, a ray of light, a vibrating chord of sound, hold within themselves the elements from which are evolved all of the sensible material forms of creation. The story of creation cannot be told, beginnings of creation cannot be reached, and the voice of a creator cannot be heard so long as these facts and potencies of the invisible world are ignored.

Upon the imponderable and intangible forces of space the foundations of the worlds are laid, and upon their currents of immeasurable velocities they are carried through the heavens in bands of reciprocal sympathy, that are so strong and enduring that earth's inhabitants cannot distinguish between rest and motion.

In following the guidance of these first things in matter and power the writer may seem to have trenched upon holy ground, and some devout minds may think him undevout, but he has learned to regard all things holy where Nature gives the imprint of her flying feet and her sensitive touch. He sees no occasion to fear rebuke for pressing thought into the presence of Him whose only perfect revelation of Himself can be made through His works, and if human thought is an image in the likeness of Divinity, the highest evidence of Sonship can be gained only by thus entering into fellowship with the Great Father. Sackcloth and ashes may be put on as symbols of worship, but a smiling face and a cheerful confidence in the daily providence of material forces are far more becoming the worshiper and a better evidence of fellowship between the human and divine than any form of sacrifice, or any symbols of humility.

This work has not been prepared in the interest of any sect of religious worshipers, neither is it desired to antagonize any class or school of philosophy. Its place among the moral forces of an advancing civilization, and upon human faith in immortality, has been earnestly considered, and the conviction of the author is, that, to those who accept its philosophy of thought, there will come a lifting up of soul after the higher possibilities of a true life, for its own sake. The bitterness and arrogance of religious sects will seem unworthy of a passing thought, save to be deplored. The thought of covering a corrupt life by shining garments, obtained by human penitence and abject beggary, so as to fit the moral leper for a happy immortality, will be banished the hope.

The fear of an angry God and the consciousness of a degraded humanity out of mind, will rid life of half its horrors, and multiply abundantly its hopes and possibilities in the real conflicts of life. Superstitious fears will pass away, and the gyves and chains forged by the leaders of men for holding the masses in subjection to mental serfdom, under the teachings of old superstitions, will fall from weary limbs as by divine deliverance. Mental culture and material purity will become the watchword of the friends of humanity and society will seek a material heaven upon earth as a preparation for a better state in the hereafter.

Self-help will be looked upon as the only way up the shining stairs of a hopeful and glorified life. To any reader of these pages who may seek in them freedom from moral restraint and a license to criminal indulgence, there will come the conviction that the material body is a self-registering tablet that is indelibly impressed with its own records of criminal indulgences, that will hold each soul to the daily fellowship of its true self, thus delineated.

Every fresh imprint of a depraved life is a new wound inflicted upon self that knows no healing, and every step of progress made in the downward road of degradation leads to a prison house that has no gates opening from without, through which deliverance can come. A debauched life, like a diseased body, is not an article of merchandise that can be bought and sold in the markets. Contracts may be made and prices paid, but no transfers are possible. If restoration can be gained, it must be only by a toilful ascent up a rugged path of earnest toil.

The hope of immortality is not shut out by the philosophy of the unseen world here presented. The two worlds are here revealed as jointly material, and as necessary to each other, as power to machine, as life to body, but the presence of mentality and personality of intellectual and moral being must be considered from a higher plane of thought than can be reached in the school of physics. We can only carry the analogy forward from this life, and assume that as materiality and mentality are co-working entities here, so they must continue to be in the hereafter. Again, it may be assumed, that in the joining of the here with the hereafter, as the physical body perishes the phantom body—that is to the physical as the electro-magnetic body is to the magnet—may enfold the mental personality within itself and take on the higher form of life, so much desired. In such a case it may follow that the fellowship of the here may not be separated from the fellowship of those that have taken on a new life.

In the preparation of these pages the writer must acknowledge some pressure above self that has held his mind for more than ten years to the subject in hand. Often the task has been laid aside and as often resumed, until with great reluctance he commits his work to thoughtful readers in the hope that errors may not be magnified, and whatever truths may here be found, become the opening door to a better knowledge of the here, with a surer trust respecting the coming life.

THE AUTHOR.

CHAPTER I.

LAWS AND MODES OF MOTION.

FROM THE SEEN TO THE UNSEEN—FROM THE SENSIBLE TO
THE REAL, TRANSCENDING, SENSIBLE RECOGNITION—
FROM THE HERE TO THE EVERYWHERE—GIVING
REVELATIONS OF THE INFINITE THROUGH
THE FINITE.

THE standpoint of sensible measures, to the student of science, is finite, and all his standards of weights and measures are inadequate to imparting any true conceptions of the infinite: Revelations from the infinite to the mind of the learner must come in such symbols as may be translated clearly into intelligent symbols of thought. The discoveries of science derive their great value from the instruction they convey respecting fixed and unvarying laws of nature, according to which the order and progressive work of a sensible creation became possible.

Into the constant working presence of physical forces the true teacher in science must lead his pupils and as he does, the assurance is gained that these forces do work according to universal laws of guidance. Schools of scientific thought will become uniform when these fixed laws of the physical forces are discovered and their working presence in nature accurately delineated.

Whatever place an infinite mind may occupy in the work of creation one thing is certain : All creative work has come into place under the fashioning potency of physical forces, and such forces as now appear, in the hands of the mechanic, as mechanical powers. Laws of motion are fixed by the impressed energy of affections of matter in lines of a constant impulse. In all the changes of matter, whether of state or place, there is perfect order and the ultimates of motion are perfections of time periods, and complete harmony of elements and bodies of matter in motion.

Laws of motion are also laws of work that belong to matter in its finest elementary states. The laws of the worlds are the same as those of the atoms out of which the worlds are built and the forces that move one also move the other. Molecular and planetary forces must have their places under the universal laws of motion, while the order of world creation must be in an ascending series from the least to the greatest.

Unseen atoms and intangible forces, are the commanding beginnings that antedate the first day of creative work. These also are native to the cold and darkness, and they encompass the entire field of thought vision. Energy, force, motion, are necessary to sensation and alone reveal material phenomena. First things to the student in all physical research are the seen, while first things in both spiritual and material sources of being are the unseen.

The scientist's line of work is unproved by way of analysis and experiment with matter in its sensible forms, to matter in its unseen and elementary states. In his entire line of investigation matter is found in charge of material forces and he is not made acquainted with a single atom devoid of energy, and I think there is nothing in the work of experiment that can lead him to believe that energy has an existence apart from elements of matter.

The scientist who treats of heat as a mode of motion has no test he can apply to matter, destitute of energy and existing as a mere passive element in Nature. If heat affords no tests revealing a material basis it has definite lines of work and gives tests of matter under the impulse of highest tension of material energy. It is light and heat that give the sublime plane of creative work where living organisms find birth and where the true history of creation can be studied in the presence of the unseen sovereignty that causes light to come forth from the darkness and life to spring out of the earth.

Light and heat are to matter, as life and thought are to the brain, and nervous system that gives to the brain its sensations, and it does not answer the purpose of the higher planes of thought to treat the lines of their influence, over matter, as simply modes of motion. There is a somewhat that binds matter to an unseen energy and gives force to material agencies that move matter and work out the myriads of form and life.

It is with this somewhat that scientific thought must seek an acquaintance, before it can solve the problem of creation, from a material standpoint, that will command universal acceptance. To do this we must rise above the testimony of the senses, and make discoveries in the realms of thought, under the guidance of careful experiments, in which the working presence of the unseen elements of material forces, that hold matter in charge, may appear, and the order of their work be diagrammed and made real to intellectual vision.

Errors in schools of science have found place and given bias to the teachings of our best masters, because of the false testimony of the senses. These errors must be sought out, and eliminated from our methods of thought, before science can make its greatest discoveries.

We still speak of the sun as rising and setting, and this accords with sensible phenomena, while scientific thought regards the sun as neither rising nor setting, but shedding upon the earth a constant light, through which the inhabitants of the central zones pass, at a distance of more than twelve thousand miles from morning to evening, and yet experiencing no sensible motion.

The three laws of motion, of our schools of philosophy, given as first truths of physical science, when brought under review, are silent respecting the nature of those forces that impress matter and establish the paths of planetary motion, giving to the planets their grand velocities, and regulating their time periods of revolution with the precision of the most perfect models of machinery in the shop of the mechanic.

The first law of motion affirms the existence of a body, as though it is self-existent, in these words: "*Every body continues in its state of rest, or of uniform motion, in a straight line, except in so far as it may be compelled by impressed forces, to change that state.*"

This initial step, in the investigation of the laws of

matter, leads us to the contemplation of bodies of matter existing without law, and independent of any innate energy, or any outward moving force. This affirmation, of the existence of matter in a state of inertia, has been the stumbling block of science all along the ages. In the analysis of matter, there are constant, and even startling revelations of energy, that take on the clothing of material forms, and appear as forces moving and conditioning matter, changing its state, and, at the same time, no dead or inert bodies of matter are discovered, and no forms of matter appear moving under the innate impulse of inertia, or of a dead weight.

While all states of matter, from its unseen atomic state to its world forms, as suns and planets, and its systems of worlds, are found in the constant keeping of innate and never changing forces; and while space is traversed with lines of force, such as light and gravity, having velocities transcending the measures of thought, with a constant conservation of all identities of being and all orders of creative work in their constant keeping, this law of inertia, conditioning matter in its beginnings to bodies at rest, without power to change their state of rest, and, if set in motion, without power to reverse or change its motion, confronts all students of physical phenomena, as an unquestioned fundamental law of physics, or, more accurately speaking, as a phenomenon without law.

Again: This dead weight of matter assumes its place as a law of motion from its persistence of continuance in a straight line, after having been set in motion by some miraculous projectile impulse, and becomes the centrifugal force, balancing gravital attraction in all planetary matter, and thus dead weight is translated into constant projectile force, as real as the force of gravity.

The second law of motion introduces a second force to account for the change of straight line motion into curve-linear lines of motion, in these words: "*Change of motion is proportional to the impressed force, and takes place in the direction of the straight line in which the force acts.*

With these laws of motion, fully in mind, there is first taught the passivity, or inertia of matter, and, in the second place, the miraculous projectile impulse of bodies of matter in a straight line; third, a change of motion by an impressed force in a straight line in the direction in which the force acts, and fourth, curve-linear motion as a compromise line of motion as a result of two independent, straight line impulses.

If it was possible that these conditions of matter and force could have place in the universality of matter and space it would be possible to individualize the conditioning impulses and guidance given to inert bodies of matter, and at the same time constituting them conditioning impulses of universal matter and universal motion, that, in their continuance, should become universal laws of motion. In short, it would be possible to show how a material universality should be conditioned by two centralized individualities, one giving straight line projective impulse, not belonging to matter, the other drawing from a centralizing, point, within matter; the former becoming continuous, through the innate inertia of matter and the other continuous by means of a constant impressing, or attracting, force from matter.

Let it be supposed that two bodies of matter, at rest in space, receive their straight line projectile impacts, at the same time, and in the same direction, and that each body, at the same time, should become an impressing central force. Both bodies would be drawn from their rectilinear line on curvelinear lines, approaching each other, and, were they moving on parallel lines, their changed lines of motion would, according to the statement of the law, be in direct lines, in the direction of their central impressing forces, and, consequently, they would be drawn on constantly converging lines that would meet at the same point in space. Such point would become an attracting center with an indeterminate line of motion, with an aggregating attracting power equal to the joint attracting energy of the two bodies. Thus the initial projectile force would be merged into central attracting energy, and the primary duality of motion, and of force, would be lost in the conjoined bodies of matter.

Again: Were all bodies of inert matter in space to receive projectile force, as an endowment from a single commanding fiat, and were all such bodies also possessed of attracting energy, their lines of motion would be as disastrous to all laws of motion as colliding bodies would be to their individual identities.

There would be, in the inaugurating of such a system of impulses, giving motion to the inert bodies of matter, no whence and no whither, no determinate centers of motion and no lines of guidance, and the mystery of the origin of inert bodies of matter in space, would be greater than the endowments of impulses subsequently given. Bodies of matter having a chaotic condition in space, inert, at rest, destitute of either innate attraction or exterior impulse of motion, present, to the thoughtful student of nature, a dead universe, pervaded by material bodies of inorganic matter, uncaused and unmoved; and, consequently antedating a first cause.

This dead universe of chaotic bodies of matter is the ideal beginning of a universe of organic matter, wrought upon and moved by creative forces, which our teachers of theology and our old masters in science have relied upon as the beginning of thought, as first truths to be accepted as fixing the standpoints of observation, that overlook the progressive unfoldments of matter into revolving worlds, illuminated and permeated by constantly working forces, giving to matter individuality of forms and material births into life.

It will be seen, at a glance, that the ideal universe of inert matter of the old masters cannot be gathered under the field glass of the astronomer, or any of its parts made subject to the test of the chemist; it cannot be measured or analyzed.

It is impossible to describe matter separate from the forces that prevade it, or the impressing forces that fix its lines of motion and establish within it the perennial fountains of life. Scientific thought cannot accept of assumptions respecting matter in an elementary state, separate from those impressing forces that give to matter its changes of state and its sublime velocities.

In the entire field of scientific investigation there are no reliable data from which we can determine the possible existence of bodies of matter, separate from impressing forces, and hence the assumed state of rest of bodies of matter, in their elementary beginnings, may safely be questioned, even in the presence of the fact that two out of the three laws of motion of our text books of philosophy are based upon the assumption.

The testimony of the senses is our authority for believing in the inertia of matter, while the testimony of scientific experiment is our authority for believing in the material forces that fix, in matter, all its states of both rest and motion.

We have already hazarded the thought that scientific methods of experiment only lead to ultimates of force, and, we may here add, to such ultimates of force as transcend sensible measure. The sovereign forces of light, heat, gravity, electricity and magnetism are classed by themselves as imponderable forces, because the most delicately poised scales of the experimenter fail to detect, in their paths of motion, the least disturbance of the balance. At these boundaries of physical phenomena, scientific thought has heretofore been baffled in all its efforts to discover the sources of the wonderful powers of these forces over matter, both affecting its states and determining its modes of motion.

As to the materiality of these forces we have the best of authority for both affirming and denying. When classed as imponderable, they were regarded as material, but in the refinement of reasoning, in our modern schools of science, it has become popular to surrender all questions, as to their materiality of structure, to the descriptive phenomena which they present, as "modes of motion."

The truth is that the problem of the forces that impress matter, fix its lines of motion and orders of organic work cannot be solved so long as dead, inert matter is treated as a necessary factor of the problem. All scientific discoveries lead to the contemplation of organic matter, as in the constant keeping of the innate affinities of atoms for atoms and the all comprehensive affinity of revolving worlds for the central suns, that give fixed laws of motion to universal matter, grouped into social systems of universal harmony of motion.

Chemical affinities and universal attraction of gravitation are nothing without matter, and, at the same time, every line of motion, of either atoms or worlds, is determined by the conditioning sovereignty of these forces.

Another thought, deserving notice, is that, as these forces cling to matter in body, so may matter, in its finest atomic, or elementary forms, cling to these forces, giving metallic lines of force to the medium environing the organic bodies that have taken on form around gravital centers.

The force currents of the magnet, environing the hardened steel that has been saturated with magnetic force, are as sensitive to metallic touch as the steel of the magnet. The magnetic field, over which a magnet extends its attractions, is pervaded by fine lines of metallic strength that reveal the same control of fine elements of iron that belongs to the steel of the magnet. The systematic arrangement of fine particles of iron around the poles of a magnet, when spread upon plane surfaces, within the fields of its influence, is secured by forces that are superior to the magnet, and, apart from it, and that brings to the steel a power of sensation that, in the case of the finely balanced magnetic needle, fixes its lines of rest, under the superior electrical currents of guidance that encircle the earth as a vast magnet.

We do not here refer to the magnet for the purpose of discussing questions of electro-magnetic energy, but simply to fix attention upon an organized, systematically working field of force currents, outside of matter, that are superior to matter and that have power to determine its lines of rest and its modes of motion. Let the thought be clearly fixed in the mind that imponderable, electromagnetic force currents, moving in space, under the guidance of a localized center, such center being a gravital center of an organic body of solid matter, represent a universal materializing potency that is a conditioning sovereignty, alike over both matter and space. This potency is now revealing itself to both the artisan and the scientist as a universal sovereignty of materialization. Matter is transparent to this sovereignty of space, and, while it is without weight, and as immeasurable as the field of the forces, it establishes the foundation centers of all organic bodies of matter and is the balancing agency of all world velocities.

CHAPTER II.

FIRST THINGS.

NO age has had such teachers as the present, and yet no age has been less confident in its elementary sources of knowledge. In physical science, in religious faith, and in the science of government, there is a prevailing feeling of unrest. The old seems to be passing away, ancient beliefs are fading under the tests of advancing knowledge, while foundations for new and better guides of thought and of life do not come into place.

Under this condition of unrest and earnest reaching forth toward the future, for surer elements of thought, and purer systems of faith, nothing that awakens partisan strife can be deserving acceptance. While earnest and faithful inquiries respecting elements of being and of life can not fail to be attacked by zealous defenders of old fables, and, experimenters with merely sensible phenomena.

Unfortunately, schools of scientific thought are restrained from making thorough search into the sources of Nature's lines of creative energy, as it is regarded by even cultured religious teachers as holy ground. The sources of light, the whence of matter, and the where of the beginning, and the when that Mind-energy was, and creation was not, it is regarded as profane to inquire after.

The writer of these pages has been restrained for years by the barrier to scientific thought and experiment that is thus thrown across the pathway of human reason in its effort to gain an acquaintance with matter and material energy in the elementary process of creation's grand work of natural unfoldment.

But the where of an intelligent creator, and the whence and what of matter, can only be sought out by parallel lines of research, and all classes of teachers, that tell us about a creator, must trace such lines of thought up to material beginnings, through material unfoldments. Ignorance respecting the latter, surely can be no evidence of wisdom respecting the former.

Prophecy respecting a creator must begin where experiment with material phenomena ends. Again: Evidences of a creator can find no place where no creation is, and mind-images of a creator can give no testimony of a self-eternity of mind, as a unit, dwelling alone with chaos and darkness. It will, therefore, rest with all those who may regard our work and methods of thought as profane, to follow us in our lines of research, respecting the elementary sources of matter and of life, to beginnings that are actual and efficient in creative work, and evolve therefrom evidences of mind-energy that may be co-existent with matter and the first things of creation, and then, if they can, tell us more about God, and the world of thought will be pleased to regard their testimony.

The experimental work of science has made us acquainted with forms of matter and material energy that reach to the grandest conceptions of the Hebrew poet, respecting the creator, when he says in the 104th Psalm, "O Lord, my God, thou art very great; thou art clothed with honor and majesty; who coverest thyself with light as with a garment; who stretchest out the heavens like a curtain; who layeth the beams of his chambers in the waters; who maketh the clouds his chariot; who walketh upon the wings of the wind; who maketh his angels spirits; his ministers a flaming fire; who laid the foundation of the earth that it should not be removed forever."

In this glowing imagery of the psalmist, there is revealed the grand potency of matter wrapped around with its own garments of light, and sending forth its ministers of fire from its cloudy chariots. With this wonderful material potency science has come into intimate fellowship. It is making merchandise of its garments of light, and its messengers wait around all our marts of trade, and go everywhere at the bidding of human thought.

Now, our thought is that a divine mind is not thus degraded by the work of science, but matter and material agencies are ennobled and made fit clothing and effective mediums of intimate fellowship between infinites of mind and infinitesimals of form, compassing all in one grand unity of being. With these glimpses of thought in vision, it may be safe for us to affirm that matter is immortal in its elements, and that the material energy that "laid the foundations of the earth, that it should not be removed forever," has always held the elements of matter well in its keeping, insomuch that chaos never had place at the world's beginnings and that a mass of dead, inert matter never was built into the world's foundation. Neither is there any point in space that is untouched with elements of material guidance.

We make these statements here not to claim the reader's acceptance, but to be kept in mind in the perusal of these pages, so as to avoid misinterpretation of our language, or of our philosophy of thought. We think our conclusions have been reached, under the guidance of masters, that have the minds of thinking men in this age, well in keeping, and who are leading them to the discovery of secrets in the domain of material being and life, that have been hidden, from the foundations of the world.

In the London, Edinburg and Dublin Philosophical Magazine, for July, 1872, Mr. James Croll, upon the theme, "What determines molecular motion?" says: "It is an opinion that is daily gaining ground that at some future time, perhaps not far distant, all the purely physical sciences will be brought under a few general laws and principles." However wide and diversified physical phenomena may seem at first sight, and however great and radical the apparent distinction between the several sciences, yet, to the eye of the thoughtful physicist, who sees deeper into the subject, they begin to appear as but the varied modifications of a few common principles.

For example: heat, electricity and magnetism are, in their ordinary phenomena, very unlike each other, yet modern investigation has shown that they are mutually convertible. Heat can be converted into electricity and electricity into magnetism. Magnetism can be converted into electricity and electricity into heat. This indicates that these corresponding sciences are not radically distinct, that their phenomena have a common origin, that in each we have the same force, manifested under different forms. To arrive at unity among the facts of Nature, has ever been, and ever will be. the aim of physical investigation.''

Again: I find in Professor Tyndall's Lectures on Light these words: "In the process of crystallization, Nature first reveals herself as a builder. Where do her operations stop? Does she continue by the play of the same forces to form the vegetable, and afterwards the animal? Whatever the answer to these questions may be, trust me that the notions of the coming generations regarding this mysterious thing, which some have called 'brute matter,' will be very different from those of the generation past." In the same line of thought we hope to make some progress, believing that by learning more about matter and its methods of world-building, we shall advance in the right line of progress towards an acquaintance with the creator.

The popular argument of first cause as a beginning in the work of creation, we regard as fallacy, from the fact that the power of causation can have no existence apart by itself. Thus placed, it is not a cause, and, when result follows cause, it must proceed out from the cause, or influence an entity outside of itself. In the former case, the cause must include all possible results, in the latter case, the effect is as much a part of the causative as is the cause. Neither can exist without the other. *A duality of causative forces*, therefore, must logically be the sources of all being, and such causative duality of all organic unity in creative work, is awaiting discovery.

Causes hide themselves in the things caused, and hence without the existence of the caused, there is not only a lack of evidence of a causative existence, but such existence could be nothing more than mere continuance. Those conceptions of matter that are limited by sensible material measures, such as magnitude, form, impenetrability and inertia, are conceptions of matter as it appears after it has passed under the fashioning touch of creative forces. These conceptions all have material boundaries and are gained by experimental tests of properties and qualities that report themselves to the senses of the experimentor. But all tests of matter wrought into sensible forms, fail to elicit any testimony respecting the history of creative potencies that have fashioned them, or of the sources from which they have been gathered, or the periods of their transformations, antedating the possession of present properties and qualities. There is no language of creation, that man has yet discovered, capable of revealing, in symbols that may be known and read of all men, the true story of the creation of the heavens and the earth.

The alphabet of creation's history must be sought out from the working presence of those unseen forces that fashion and modify the properties of bodies of matter giving them place and motion, fixed, uniform and unchanging in their orders of succession, while they, as forces, hide themselves in the elementary forms of matter that move with the velocity of light and keep company with the sunbeam in carrying forward the beneficent work of giving seed time and harvest to all worlds in the sun's system, and clothing them all with the changing drapery of an eternal creating potency.

As we have seen from highly respected authority that gravitation, heat, light, magnetism and electricity may be converted into each other, we take but a single step forward in scientific thought in affirming that they are all modifications of one sovereign force, having a duality of expression that we here designate as attraction and repulsion. Light, heat, electricity, magnetism and gravitation, when fully understood, will alike give us the backward and forward motion of attraction and repulsion, while each will also reveal a constant right angled cross section of forces that give circular paths to the planets, and spherical form to all worlds, and all seed and germ forms in all worlds. I say in all worlds, because these forces have but one testimony in their methods of work in creation on our earth and the sun and stars tell the same story of light that is told between sun and planet. Gravitation, also, binds the solar system in the strong cords of its omnipotent currents of force, and fixes the machinery of the sun's system of satellites and planets, and hence we believe it rules over a universe of worlds without a rival.

One step more we may take, in our study of the unity of creative forces, and assume that chemical affinity and gravitation are but different expressions of the same universal force. While gravitation finds expression in its control of planetary bodies, across intervening space, chemical affinity finds expression in the mysterious unfoldments of atomic forms of matter, in all sensitive organic unions. I would express my conception of the unity of these forces, as they appear under the mental visions of the astronomer and chemist, by calling them the *universal potency of sensation.*

The reach of these forces is beyond the reach of both telescope and microscope, and at the same time they reveal their omnipotence to the touch of each atomic element that enters into the myriad forms of Nature's building.

These forces must antedate all created forms of matter and they alone can reveal the periods of beginnings at which creation's work began. The foundations of all suns and planetary bodies were committed to their keeping, and they are now revealing themselves as the Alpha and Omega, the beginning and the end, of all material measures of human thought, as applied to the infinites of creation. They are the measures of space, and of those omnipotent forces that hold atoms and worlds within their embrace, constituting a material providence over every thing that has sensation and motion.

I make these statements as the very beginning of my acquaintance with the reader of these pages, because it is my purpose to simplify the problems of scientific thought, so as to make my solutions plain to the comprehension of human vision.

The time has come when scientific dreams must submit to the test of materialization, to gain the confidence of the thinking, inquiring masses. The capacity of the scientist must be measured by his efforts at translating the true language of Nature into the well studied symbols of daily life. To-day is the day of beginnings of creation, as truly as any period in the past. It is within the experience of a single life that all the mysteries of creation pass before the questioning tribunal of human reason.

The environment of child life furnishes, entire, the object lessons from which the schools of philosophy construct the most difficult problems of their text-books of science. In a single drop of sea water, we have the problem of the oceans; in a single rain drop, there is the story of the rivers; in a ray of light, the story of the sun, with his family of worlds; in the fall of an apple, the story of all world motion, and in the unfolding of life from a single germ, the story of creation, repeated from generation to generation, ever the same. The observatory of the astronomer, and the laboratory of the chemist, are simply centers of observation, and the instruments and elements of these workshops of science, are all subservient to the sensations that are centered within the dark chambers of the animal brain. The secrets of Nature, by such instrumentalities alone are disclosed and the methods of matter and material forces are revealed to intellectual vision; but still all of scientific knowledge, thus gained, is bounded by the natural sensations of a single mental environment.

Once more must be noted that the knowledge, gained by a single experimenting hand, becomes the knowledge of the world through human testimony, because these material forces, that convey sensations to the mental conceptions of a single brain, are true to Nature and always impart the same testimony to all sensatory living beings. The language of the senses is a universal language. It imparts knowledge to the lower order of animals, as truly as to man. In seeing, hearing, tasting, smelling and feeling, all animal life has a common heritage, and, by means of this common heritage, they must be regarded as units of a material creation, that is, in its completeness of infinite measures, a single unity. There is a unity between the light and the eye, that indicates their origin in the same lines of force that now give sight to the brain life.

In the ear, there is evidence that the chords of vibratory currents of force producing sound, had a companionship with the life germ in which the ear had its beginning. So all organs of sensation possess unmistakable evidence of having proceeded out of those forces that are unseen and imponderable, and that join sensatory life with sensible forms of matter. The knowledge of self and the home, in which self finds life, is the story of the garden of Eden incorporated into the life of every intellectual being. That which weaves the life out of the garden home, weaves the garden home into the life that dresses the garden, and they thus, through the sensatory touches of constant fellowship, constitute the natural boundaries of human life, and all possible sources of human wisdom. To drop all figures of speech, what I desire to say, is that the home in which a child is born, with its natural environments, possesses all necessary object lessons for the attainment of the highest possibilities of human knowledge.

Nature does her best and most complete work when she reaches the high level of self-consciousness, and such level is reached through the sensatory communion of the material forces, with the self-consciousness of the human mind. It is upon this plane of intellectual being, that every one may become a philosopher, and every philosopher gain a true knowledge of the sources of life and being. I write thus for the purpose of confining thought within the bounds of true sources of knowledge, and ruling out of scientific research, all dreams and fables of marvelous discoveries and physical wonders that find no place in the now material facts and forces of creation.

First things of creation have been assigned to a period antedating material forces, and consequently antedating all possible conditions of human knowledge.

At such a period, it is assumed that matter and darkness possessed an accidental nebulous or cosmic condition, and that a universal mind-force thus had dominion over a universe of chaotic matter, apart from, and antedating, that system of material forces that now reign in a complete sovereignty of universal creative harmony. Thus, matter, and the forces that now touch matter in its every atom, are supposed to have had separate beginnings, and to have been brought together at the beginning of a special creation. According to this hypothesis, matter was non-creative, separate from the forces and the forces have no place apart from matter.

By recognizing the unity of the forces of gravity, light, electricity and magnetism, and their now joint sovereignty over all growing forms and all revolving worlds, it follows that the beginnings of creation mark that period when matter and material forces were blended, constituting that material causality that unfolds life-forms, wherever atmosphere, light, heat and moisture give living environments.

In a logical sequence of beginnings, gravitation and darkness, magnetism and cold, securing crystalization, are first, while light, heat, electrical displays of force, are second, and yet they are companion forces, always working in a perfectly balanced unity, producing uuiform results, securing universal harmony.

In these statements respecting first things the reader will find many problems demanding solution, and many themes for lengthy dissertations.

The distinction I desire to make between matter and the material forces that move matter, have never been clearly drawn in the schools of science, while the distinctions between mind and matter are treated of in schools of theology as a basal principle of religious faith. The debasing of the flesh to purify the soul, the degrading of matter to the ennobling of the mind, and even the scourging of the body and crucifying the flesh to purify and save the soul, as inwrought into all religious life and forms of worship, all spring from a belief in the sovereignty of a mind force, to which matter is accidental, secondary, sinful, corrupt and perishing.

Hence it is that the battle ground between science and religion is simply narrowed to a hypothetical distinction between mental and material forces in their determining influences upon material organisms, having life. In the present age of scientific discovery, the supernatural takes no part in the contests of the schools. The science of theology, and the science of Nature, occupy an open field, for purely mental conflict. The gods are silent, relying solely on past utterances, while new testimony comes daily to human life, through new discoveries in the working presence of material forces. Scientific minds have hitherto been content to admit supernatural testimony to a place in their systems of philosophy, and hence have taught half truths, and thereby have failed to discover sources of creative work, and ultimates of matter, within the domain of mental vision. This statement will find ample illustration in the progress of this work, as the cases are noted, in which masters in science have failed in their loyalty to their true mission, through an undue regard for ancient testimony, having the authority of divine approval.

A single illustration of our thought will here suffice, as it will disclose the verities upon which rest the real discoveries of mental telescopic vision.

The discovery by Sir Isaac Newton, of the law of universal gravitation, was a mental necessity, based upon two facts of matter in motion, under the impulse of natural forces, namely: The fall of an apple, and the motion of a secondary body around its primary as taught by the Copernican system of astronomy. The apple, a sphere, falls to the earth on a plumb line, making one of the radii of a sphere. The planet, a sphere, one of a system of worlds, moves on a curved line, at a uniform distance from a much larger sphere that establishes the center of its orbital plane of motion. The mental conception was that matter attracts matter directly as mass, and from mathematical computation it was made appear that such attraction decreases as the square of distance increases. Thus, the presence of an unseen potency, centered in and surrounding all sun and planetary bodies, is believed in as confidently as if the force could be seen and handled, as bodies of matter are seen and handled.

But in the apple, the action of the force between it and the earth, must have been reciprocal on plumb lines toward the earth's center, while on the planet, the action commanding motion, must have been on orbital lines around the primary body.

The motions of the two bodies, in their fixed paths, disclose the presence of an environment of occult force currents around each moving sphere determining its path of motion. The force environing the apple gives its path of motion a radial line of the earth, as the larger sphere. This discloses gravital attraction of the earth's environment of forces, affecting other bodies of matter upon radial lines, attracting, as appears from experiment, alike upon all possible radial lines that may be drawn towards the earth's center. The power of the earth's attraction on such radial lines decreases as the square of distance increases. But the motion of the planet in its orbit around the sun, is across the radial lines of the sun's attraction, cutting such lines at right angles to its path of motion.

Now, by comparing the radial lines of gravity with the orbital lines of planetary motion, we find that bodies move along gravital lines with a constantly *accelerating* motion, while on orbital lines they move with a *uniform* motion. This surely teaches that gravital attraction finds, at each planet's orbital distance from the sun, a right angled force, just balancing the force of attraction, and hence the even and insensible motion of each planet in its orbit.

Again: Radial lines of gravital attractions are reciprocal lines of force, resulting in establishing a mutual communing of sun and planet, through the joint gravital environment of the two bodies, hence the gravital environment of sun and planet is an environment of gravital force currents, centrally bound to each body, exchanging impulses of restraint, under the united sovereignty of which light, heat, life and motion, at least, on the planet are conserved. The respective environments of sun and planet, have a common radial measure varying uniformly from each body inversely as the square of distance.

Sun light and earth light respect these radial lines of gravity and reveal their radiance on the surface of each body at a level where gravital potency is the greatest.

Thus the great problem of Newton's law of gravity is unfolded to mental vision. The only sensible contact gained by us of these wonderful spherical environments of force currents around earth and sun is in the vibrating linear currents of the so-called sun's rays of light. Rocks, mountains and plains, rivers, seas and oceans, vegetables, shrubs, trees and animals, are all built into place, under the unfailing providence of these benign environing forces of sun and planet. *The great deep of cold, dark, environing space is thus bridged between sun and planetary bodies by both mental vision and sensible contact.*

Under this vision of gravital planetary environment, space is not a vacuum, but rather the home of the forces, the whence of all motion, the perennial fountain, out of which come the forms of creative work, as vegetable, tree and animal, are woven out of sun forces and earth forces, establishing germ centers and unfolding all possible forms of body and of life, from their self-moved and self-organizing vibrating currents of force.

I have thus endeavored to visualize gravital forces as they take on form, in my own mind, under the discovery of Sir Isaac Newton.

But the sweep of the planets across these radial currents of the sun's gravital attraction, with a velocity like that of the earth, 1,000 miles in a minute of time reveals a companion force to that of gravity, that must have a place among the forces, giving motion to matter. The mental conception of Newton, of the force of gravity, was limited by the idea of mutual attractions between bodies of matter, and hence he made no discovery of the force in Nature, giving right angled motion to a planet in its orbit, to the radial line, joining the center of the planet with the center of the sun. He lived in an age when science was feared and fables were taught under divine sanctions, and hence he incorporated his new discovery with the conception of a divine potency, imparting to inert matter an impact, giving it straight line motion.

It seemed to him sufficient to discover in matter a law of central attractions, to fix planets in their orbits as they already had gained straight line motion from the hand that made them, hence the parallelogram of forces was a necessity in schools of philosophy, to bring together straight line divine impulse and central material forces.

This method of incorporating the incomplete work of the creator with the material force of gravity has been deemed satisfactory in all of our modern schools of science. It seems even now almost presumptuous to question the wisdom of the great masters who have, under the guidance of a Newton, taught the great law of the parallelogram of forces; and to affirm that it is but half true, that it gives us an unbalanced equation of material forces that gives to the physicist so many unsolved problems in the scientific schools of the present time. A force in matter acting on radial lines was the discovery of Newton, but the force giving orbital motion to bodies of matter seems still awaiting discovery. He caught a glimpse of that world force, that guides ponderable bodies of matter on plumb lines, in their fall towards the center of the earth; and that also holds the planets to the central sun, in their paths of revolution, on a line joining the center of each planet to the center of the sun, thus confining their paths around the sun to closed circular orbits of definite forms, accurate in time measures. Yet he seems not to have formulated any statement of his actual belief as to the nature of such force. He says: "The cause of gravity is what I do not pretend to know. It is inconceivable that inanimate brute matter should, without the mediation of something else which is not material, operate on and effect other matter without mutual contact, as it must do if gravitation be essential and inherent in it. That gravity should be innate, inherent, and essential to matter, so that one body may act upon another at a distance, through a vacuum, without the mediation of anything else, by and through which their action and force may be conveyed from one to another, is to me so great an absurdity that I believe no man who has, in philosophic matters, a competent faculty of thinking, can ever fall into it. Gravity must be caused by an agent, acting constantly according to certain laws; but whether this agent be material or immaterial, I have left to the consideration of my readers."

These statements of the great discoverer of the presence of occult forces, holding the planetary worlds in charge, indicate that he was conscious of having only entered upon the inviting field of discovery respecting those unseen forces that command matter in its ever changing states.

It will be noticed that he refers to matter as "inanimate brute matter," and to space as a supposed "vacuum," and hence, believing, as he did, in the first two laws of motion, it was utterly impossible for him to determine either the cause of gravity or its nature as an agent, "whether material or immaterial.

Clearly, matter could not be inert, and at the same time inaugurate a system of planetary worlds, binding them together by central attractions, acting across millions of miles of intervening space, and that central attraction so resisted by orbital or projectile forces as to secure orbital velocities, equal to that of the planets, finds no explanation in the inertia of bodies of matter.

But the third law of motion, a discovery by Sir Isaac Newton, indicates a reciprocal sympathy, existing between bodies of matter that conditions all their modes of motion. This law teaches that: *"To every motion there is always an equal and a contrary reaction; or, the mutual actions of any two bodies are always equal and oppositely directed in the same straight line."*

Conservation of energy and conservation of forces imparting motion, are clearly bound up in this law. Constant pulsations of force currents between bodies of matter across all distances of space, measured by the capacities of bodies to receive and give impulse, may be also derived from this third law of motion.

By this law each atom of matter, or each body of matter, has its measuring unit of force. It only gives as it receives, and receives from the vast infinites of force, strength and guidance suited to its individuality.

In the communing of bodies of matter, through acting and reacting impulses of equal currents of energy through intervening space, there is revealed a materiality of forces binding all planetary bodies, within each solar system, through the joint embrace of two equal and jointly sovereign streams of counterflowing impulses, that impart to such bodies their grand velocities, and fix all their paths of motion.

Thus, interplanetary space becomes a factor in the grand problem of world motion, that our old philosophers have entirely overlooked in formulating their mathematical problems of astronomical science. Hence, their failure to classify the imponderable forces of light, gravity, electricity and magnetism among the properties of matter. While they have given inertia as a property of bodies of matter, they have not extended their material measurements beyond the liquid elements of the oceans and these supplemented by the gaseous elements that unite in building liquids and solids from themselves. The outmost boundaries of matter, they have supposed, were reached in its gaseous state, and this leaves the vast fields of space open to scientific discovery, under the guidance of those force-currents that flow from gravital center to gravital center, of sun and planet, with the velocity of light, and bear upon their circling currents the planets in their orbits fulfilling their measured time periods of revolution.

It is logical, then, to regard the great field of planetary motion as the home of the forces that impart to the planets their grand velocities. This field is swept by a system of forces that gives stability and perfection of order to every line of motion, and directs every atom, molecule or planetary body of matter, that has its place within the field. Order reigns at every point in space, and under the sweep of these forces there is not a lawless atom, nor a dead or dying world. Chaotic, or nebulous states of matter, are not possible under the searching presence of the all pervading attractions and repulsions of these everflowing streams that pervade and encircle the systems of worlds that constitute the machinery of the heavens. When the scientific mind gains an adequate conception of the sources of materiality as ever abiding in the deep, darkly flowing floods of virgin matter of infinite space, pulsating with a universal dual energy of attraction and repulsion that is innate and immortal, in elementary forces and elementary atoms, then it will not be thought strange that space should be compassed by grand flowing streams of virgin matter, having velocities like light, and revealing a sovereignty over matter in all its states and in all its paths of motion. When Newton, in his mental vision, saw a force back of the sensible form of the apple that pulled it to the earth and fixed the line of its motion toward the earth, he disclosed a new world to the vision of the philosopher, more wonderful than that disclosed by the microscope and telescope. He saw, beyond the reach of the field glasses of science, a universal power holding both atoms and worlds in charge and fixing all laws of motion. Yet, he could not tell whether it was material or immaterial. But this he knew, the planets were held firmly in its embrace, while millions of miles of free space marked the intervals, across which this power performed constant work, as real in the revolutions of planetary worlds as the wheels in the shop of the mechanic driven by the flowing stream, or the expansive power of steam. It is clearly apparent that his belief in the first two laws of motion, clouded his vision and limited his discoveries to the law of central attractions, leaving the law of orbital revolutions to be discovered by other minds.

The discovery of universal attraction, binding suns and planets in systems of revolving worlds, is the discovery of matter in its dynamic state, as light, gravity, electricity, magnetism and chemical affinity. It is the discovery of matter in its imponderable state, as grand, flowing sovereignties of motion and of all creative work. Matter ceases to be "brute matter," and space ceases to be a "vacuum," when it puts on the clothing of light, or leaps from the dark cloud, choosing material paths of guidance, uttering a voice that declares its omnipotence; or, again, when it gathers around the iron of the electro-magnet, at the command of a passing dark and silently flowing electrical current, and lifts hundreds of pounds of "brute matter."

Matter, under these conditions, has its lines of motion and its grand velocities of infinite measures, with its births dating with the eternities and its home in universal space. With this view of elementary matter, constituting the imponderable and unseen forces, taking on the lines of rapidly flowing currents, like those of light, electricity, and magnetism, we discover the cause of the failure of our scientists to weigh the forces. They are balanced and balancing forces. They have no weight, and all matter, and all material bodies, are nicely poised upon gravital centers, that take up their grand velocities as evenly as the balancing wheels of working machinery take up motion from the push and pull of the piston rod of the invisible power that commands work from within the cylinder of the steam engine. The engineer weighs his coal and measures his wood that he casts into the furnace as a source of power. He also causes the water, as a secondary source of power, to flow into the boiler of his engine, and this, too, has its weight and measure. His purpose is to evoke power from "brute matter," that shall cause the wheels of machinery to do work as things of life, from an indwelling power of motion. To do this he must convert his wood and coal and water from their forms of material weights and measures, to new forms, that lift weights and resist measures. The highest plane of power is reached when the coal and the wood are converted into light and heat, and the water into the heated, rushing, breath of the steam-chest, that mark the vanishing line between ponderable matter and imponderable elements of matter, as force currents in their native home, free space. The wood and coal are simply frozen blocks of sunlight and gravity, and freezing is the rest point of attraction, as light and heat are the vanishing points of repulsion and motion.

Matter in its rest state is never released from the charge of matter in its elementary state. Its only rest is the grand velocities of revolving worlds; hence in its elementary or dynamic state it compasses the entire field of rest and motion, as a self-conditioning sovereignty.

I have said the engineer regards the wood and the water as sources of power, so have our old masters, in their scientific experiments, treated of matter in its organic, or rest state, as the whence of both force and forms of being. They have failed to conceive of matter, in its elementary sovereignties over both revolving worlds and free space; consequently the student's first lesson in our school of natural science commences with matter in an organic state of deadness, or inertness. The forces and their consequent velocities are represented as accidental sovereignties, coming to matter, pushing it on straight lines and pulling it on curved lines securing planetary motion. The push has been written down as a centrifugal force and the pull as a centripetal force; the former as resulting from the deadness of matter, the latter as resulting from an innate living force of attraction.

But the mechanic of to-day is evoking power from free space that is a sovereign in the presence of both fire and steam. It comes out of the cold and the darkness, binds its working center to the solid bars of soft iron forming the balancing center of dynamo machinery, and from itself gives attraction and repulsion, with velocities like those of light and gravity, and also from its infinite sources of strength pours forth constant floods of light and heat rivaling the sun in its brightness and beauty. The whence of electricity, magnetism, light and heat is thus clearly, even demonstrably revealed as from material conditions of the force currents of free space. As gravity has heretofore been regarded as an attracting potency, bound to world centers, and at the same time filling all space with its sovereign presence, determining the lines of motion and grand harmony of the machinery of the heavens, and as the old masters could not tell whether it was material or immaterial, the artisans and mechanics of our own civilization have seized upon the imponderable forces of electricity and magnetism and converted them directly into mechanical potencies, both revolving the wheels of working machinery and lighting the shops of our cities and our marts of trade. It becomes, therefore, increasingly evident that space is not a vacuum, and that those imponderable forces that have troubled our masters in science so much to classify, in their relations to matter, are sovereign over matter, holding in themselves all the possibilities of material forms and the sources of all life, with its sensations and indwelling promises of continuance. In the great circles of the forces, that give to us day and night, heat and cold, that are inwrought into all the circles of life, there is a revelation of an intimate communion between the imponderable forces of matter and the multiform evolutions of matter into living organisms. In the attraction and repulsion, the choosing and refusing of the magnet there is a sensatory organism that is more than a shadow of vegetable and animal life.

THE MAGNET.

The sensations of the magnet are an open door for mental discoveries in the invisible world. The magnet is a representative of pónderable matter and imponderable forces. It has a real body, and at the same time a phantom body of the most delicate structure revealing sensations as real and mysterious as those of light, heat and life. It has a dual organism that unites the visible world to the invisible, the organic to the inorganic, the created to the uncreated and elemental. It has in it a center of rest and at the same time chosen paths of motion. It has an individuality, and yet is a part of a grand impersonality. It marks out lines of latitude and longitude upon the earth, and also holds communion with the sun in its daily circles of light around the earth. It reports disturbances upon the body of the sun and quivers under auroral displays of light upon the earth. These statements need no proof, they are known by men of science and are open to the vision of the unlettered.

The influence of the sun upon the magnetic needle discloses so clearly the invisible sensations that influence the magnet, it is important to fix the record of such influence in every mind.

Professor Proctor has noticed this influence in a single paragraph on page 44 of his book entitled, "Other Worlds Than Ours," which is deserving careful attention. He says: "It has long been noticed that, during the course of a single day, the magnetic needle exhibits a minute change of direction taking place in an oscillating manner, and, when the character of this vibration came to be carefully examined, it was found to correspond to a sort of effort on the needle's part, to turn toward the sun. This happens twice in the day; once when the sun is above the horizon and once when he is below it. When the sun is midway between these two positions, which also happens twice in the day, the needle has its mean position, because the northern and the southern ends make equal efforts, so to speak, to direct themselves toward the sun. Four times in the day then, the needle has its mean position, or is directed toward the magnetic meridian. But, when the sun is not in one of the four positions considered, that end of the needle which is nearest to him is slightly turned away from its mean position toward him.

The change of position is very minute, and only the exact modes of observation made use of in the present age would suffice to reveal it. There it is, however, and this minute and seemingly unimportant peculiarity has been found to be full of meaning."

This behavior of the needle under the influence of the sun clearly teaches that the combination of forces that seems to hold the needle in charge on its pivotal bearing holds the worlds in charge upon their central bearings in the great plane of the ecliptic; and also that their polar bearings and paths of motion are under the directing guidance of the same forces.

The earth and needle have each a phantom body of currents of force that give them rest and motion. Their phantom bodies are individualized around a magnetic center in matter in its ponderable forms, and yet are under each other's constant sympathy and directive guidance. The sun also has his phantom body of forces, and across the 92,000,000 of miles separating earth from sun, he holds communion with both earth and needle, with a directive guidance over them as real as the beams of light that come and go under his directive presence.

Clearly the highways of the forces of the magnet are across the great intervals of space separating sun and planets. So the highways of light are across the same dark reaches of distance, and may it not be possible that the forces of the magnet and of the sunbeams are a unit in conferring light, heat and motion upon earth and sun? Sensations go with these forces between sun and earth; attractions and repulsions touch the magnetic needle and earth with their constantly varying influences coming from the sun, while the sensations of light and heat are given and withheld by the seeming coming and going of the sun in his daily circuits in the heavens. It seems as if these forces have bridged the great chasms separating sun and planets with a structure of material forces that are as real and enduring as the steel of the magnet or the rock-ribbed foundations of the earth.

It may be asked respecting the whence of sun and planets and the whence of the forces that encircle and uphold them, did the sun and planets antedate the forces in the order of their coming, or did the forces antedate the worlds that are made? Or, to vary the query, did creation antedate the creator? or did the creator antedate creation? The men who have dealt most successfully with the problem of planetary motion have felt deeply the importance of discovering some law of material forces that would account for the grand velocities of the planets in their fixed orbits of motion.

I find a statement in Professor Mitchel's class-book on astronomy in which he says: "Kepler, whose fertile genius, ever active and untiring, sought the cause of planetary motion, and, being ignorant of the laws of motion, felt that he must discover and reveal some constantly active power operating in the direction of planetary motion so as to keep up the velocity, believing that, without some such ever active force the planets must of necessity stop.

"The successors of Kepler and Galileo, for fifty years, or during the first half of the seventeenth century, felt strongly the necessity of a physical theory of the planetary motions without attaining to anything clear or satisfactory."

This strongly felt necessity of a theory of physical forces based upon well known laws of material energy, outside of and superior to organic matter, would be still felt, were it not for the discovery of Sir Isaac Newton of the law of universal gravitation, supplemented by the laws of motion that have gained a place in our schools of philosophy as accounting for the motion of the planet in its orbit.

Scientific minds have rested in the belief that ultimates have been reached in this field of astronomical science, and discovery ceased. But a new light has come to us from world forces as they are revealed in the magnet and electro-magnet, and if we will but follow its guidings it will lead us securely to the discovery of forces that are sovereign over matter, and as universal in their possibilities as space is in its measures.

The magnet gives to the scientist of to-day its magnetic field of material force-currents that has in it all of the potencies systematically fixed in their methods of work; that are necessary to give to sun and planets centers of rest and orbits of motion, confirming the Copernican system of planetary motions. What Kepler earnestly sought after has come to our teachers in science unsought, and their eyes seem to be holden that they should not see it.

CHAPTER III.

THE MYSTERIES OF THE MAGNET.

THE sensible revelations of the magnet are centered in a dual evolution of material energy, and such energy appears at the poles of the magnet as attraction and repulsion. These two classes of energy are reciprocal and equal, and appear alike at either pole. Their sources of supply are exhaustless and constant. Their strength may be accumulated by mechanical devices, and be strengthened by mechanical disturbances. Friction which retards the development of power from other sources serves to develop strength as an accumulator of energy from the working forces that are stored up in the magnet.

Experiments with the magnet have revealed the presence of electrical phenomena in silent currents of electricity that flow around it. These currents in a permanent magnet, could they be seen as represented in figure 1, by a person looking towards the south pole, would appear to flow from left to right, and to one looking toward the north pole they would seem to reverse and flow from right to left. These currents consequently cross the magnetic needle at right angles to the north and south

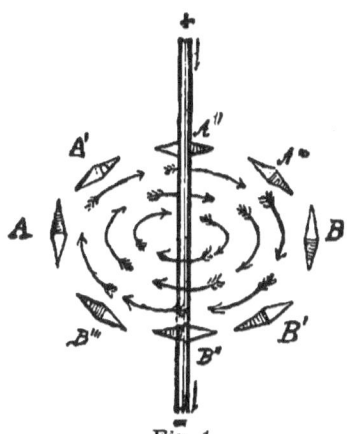

Fig. 1.

axial lines of its natural position of rest upon a pivotal bearing parallel to the magnetic meridian of the earth. The magnetic needle reveals the presence of these currents by its behavior in the presence of a passing electric current. The discovery of electric currents crossing the magnet was made by Œrested in the first quarter of the present century. He noticed that "a magnetic needle always tends to place itself at right angles to a wire carrying a current of electricity," (see Fig. 2,) "and that the

Fig. 2.

north pole of the needle was deflected to the right or left, according to the direction of the current, and according to whether the wire was placed above or below the needle. In the figure the arrows show that when the current passes over the needle coursing from its north pole in the direction of its south pole, the needle will swing so as to turn its north pole east and its south pole west of the line; if the wire passes beneath instead of above the needle the direction of swing would be reversed." By passing the current from south to north the results would be reversed.

Thus it will appear that the magnetic needle is held in its position upon the earth by the flow of electric currents at right angles to its polar bearings on a meridian line of the earth, and that the electric currents that pass around the earth as a great magnet from east to west, by coinciding in the line of their flow with those passing below the magnet, cause it to come to rest on the earth's magnetic meridian.

But as I have represented the flow of the currents, it should be noticed that the currents flow around the north pole of the earth from east to west, while upon the upper side of the needle they flow from west to east, and on the under side from east to west. This arises from the fact that the so-called north pole of the needle is a south pole in the flow of its currents when compared with the currents of the earth. But by placing a north pole over a north pole they would repel each other, as the currents passing between the two magnets of earth and needle would flow in opposite directions; hence a reversal of poles by the needle in such an event always occurs. This gives rise to the law of magnetic phenomena, that likes repel likes and opposites attract. North poles attract south poles, and south poles north poles, and only thus, whether placed side by side or end to end.

Thus we trace back the attracting and repelling power of the magnet to the commanding sources of its strength in the electric currents that flow in orbital currents around it, and at all times at right angles to the flow of magnetic attracting currents.

The mysterious power of the magnet is then an evolution out of the great currents of material forces that reveal themselves in ponderable matter, flowing from outlying fields of immeasurable space. They are a sovereign power in matter, though doing work outside of it in grand orbital floods circling around it. The most wonderful aggregations of matter in body, consisting of worlds and sun-systems of worlds, are encircled with the directive lines of these electric currents, while such bodies are saturated with the central bindings of gravital or magnetic attractions.

The little magnetic needle and the great earth agree in obeying the coercive currents of their immediate presence, while the far off planets and the central sun are revolved and attracted by one universal binding of sympathy that seems to disclose the circling currents of these same great potencies in the fixed paths of the planets in their perpetual journeyings around the central sun.

The great laws of planetary motion are evidently the same as the laws of currents and magnets, in their influence over each other. If electric currents move around the sun and planets, parallel to the plane of the ecliptic, and electric currents move around the magnet at right angles to the same, the equatorial plane of the magnet and its polar positions with reference to such plane, will be similar to the positions of sun and planets in the great plane of the ecliptic.

As the magnetic needle takes up its position upon the earth, with poles reversed to those of the earth, the larger magnet, so all of the planets take up their positions with reference to the sun, the great magnet of the solar system, with poles reversed to those of the sun, and hence the great flow of both sun currents and earth currents between the two bodies is in the same direction. They move in concert and mutually attract each other, binding the two bodies to each other in responsive sympathy, and in bonds of ceaseless activity and unfailing energy.

The great law of attraction, as revealed in electrical currents, is that those flowing in the same direction attract each other, while repulsion is developed when they meet each other flowing in opposite directions.

This law applies to currents of the same class. Positive currents unite when flowing in the same directions, while negative currents unite in flowing in opposite directions to the positive. The balance of all current motion is preserved in the unit measure of force, consisting of pairs, one positive and one negative line of energy, moving in opposite directions to each other, and bound, each to each, by some lateral sympathy. It is the equal sympathy, or attractive energy, of these two lines of currents, constituting a unit of force that compels closed circuits in all tranference of energy in lines of motion. There must be a to and from in straight lines or an around in orbital lines to maintain current motion according to electrical phenomena. Magnetic energy does its work in right lines of to and from, while electrical energy does its work in orbital lines around in closed circles. These two classes of energy work together around a common center, and hence in the grand flow of their currents *they must cross each other at right angles.* These two classes of energy, flowing in currents, give us the companion forces that unite in a common field, around a common center, to give power to the metallic structure of the magnet.

The phenomena of magnets and currents, that I have attempted to combine so as to gain a mental vision of the two forces of electricity and magnetism in their normal methods of combination, giving power to the magnet, find a material contrivance in the electro-magnet, that, to my own mind, materializes these forces in their separate lines of work and individualizes them in their joint combinations for evoking power. The physicist, who, by battery and insulated wire, brings invisible forces to the iron core of the electro-magnet, and notes the displays of power that are thus obtained, cannot fail to note the presence of a material sovereignty over matter in these imponderable forces. The electro-magnet is of such great importance in the working of the telegraph and the telephone and in the developing of electricity for electric lighting that it scarcely needs a description, and yet, for the purpose of ascending to higher planes of thought, writer and reader must gain a true interpretation of symbols of invisible forces that are wrought into the material structure of the magnet, so as to gain a true conception of the phantom body of material form that comes and goes at the making and breaking of the circuit that joins magnet and battery.

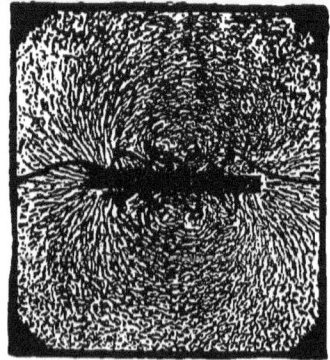

Fig. 3.

A wire, wound with thread or silk so as to restrain a current of electricity from passing off by contact with another metal, if wound around a bar of soft iron, in a continuous coil from end to end, and the terminals of the wire united to the conjunctive wires of a voltaic battery, will form an electro-magnet. Figure 3 represents such a magnet. The lines of magnetic impulse, given to the magnet by the current coursing through the wire, are visualized in the lines of iron filings that, spread upon a paper plane above the magnet, have become magnetic, under the guidance of magnetic lines of force. The little particles of iron become magnets and join together by polar forces, making lines that indicate the tendency of magnets to impart of their magic energy to other bodies of matter, fixing a bond of sympathy between them. These little magnets take up uniform lines of rest, and, like lines of soldiers, show in all of their evolutions the command of some superior influencing agency. The commanding electrical currents, flowing around the core of the magnet are unseen, but where the lines of magnets appear best defined, and clustered as stalks of grain grown up for the sickle of the reaper, from the magnet as from the earth, there, it is safe to affirm, electric currents are passing at right angles to the magnetic lines. More than this, they are moving in circles around each line of magnets. Thus the disturbed magnets appear as things of life, under the command and inflowing energy of unseen potencies from their own environment of place in a field of forces that take on strength and diversity of individualities from a whence beyond the reach of the senses. Thus in the magnet, the world of sensation and the sub-sensible world of infinite creative potencies, are joined together by material bonds of an immortal texture. Here the creator and the created meet face to face, and here, if scientist and theologian must worship, they can discover the revealed presence of the everlasting I Am, the creator of the heavens and the earth.

We must here center thought where Nature centers power, and begins creative work, and takes up her paths of motion. Catechise the electric forces as we may, they are the sources of all creative power, and hold in charge the atoms of the substances that now appear in world-forms. The chosen paths of these forces are not straight lines, but circles; their chosen forms are not many-sided figures, but spheres. Their true measures are from centers of rest to orbital paths of motion. Their units are atoms and the dual balanced lines of the sunbeam and the oppositely moving lines of the electric current.

As we have referred to the power of the magnet as resting within the creative energy of the current flowing through the encircling wire of the magnet, and the power of the entire magnetic field, as a revelation of strength from the same source of power, it becomes necessary to emphasize the fact that orbital currents are first things in Nature's lines of motion. The backward flow of the electric current is always equal to its forward flow, and there is neither a forward or backward flow without a completed circuit, and a completed circuit is an orbital line partaking of the elements of a circle. Hence, the electric current works so kindly in the electro magnet, and delivers its strength so persistently to straight lined currents in magnets that centralize force and act and react on radial lines.

A magnetic sphere as constructed out of magnets and circles, would have all of its radial lines magnets, and all of its curved lines electrical currents; hence a gravital force is a magnetic force, and binds magnets to magnets, while a repulsive orbital force is an electrical force that creates magnetic bodies and adjusts all paths of sympathetic intercourse between them in obedience to gravital bindings.

The behavior of magnets in the field of a passing current is seen in the phantom of its creation, under filings given in Fig. 4. At the right and left of the passing current the filings have left a light field from which they have gone at the bidding of the current, and have laid themselves at rest at right angles to the passing current. Were

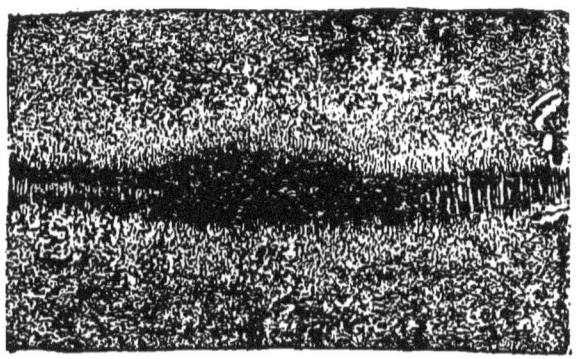

Fig. 4.

the current bent into the form of a circle, all of the filings would rest on the current as radial lines would cut it. Such magnets increased in length and strength would become radial to the circle and extend outward to the field of space influenced by the passing current.

It should be kept in mind that currents create, and that all magnetic lines of attraction are simply centralizing potencies created and controlled by, electrical orbital currents that are from the great deep of infinite space. These currents are held to the ponderable magnetic body of sun or planet by magnetic attraction, while they at every point of their flow as currents tend to pass outward from the body, as a stone held by a string when swung around the head would tend at every point of motion to pass outward from the restraint of the string. But as the radial magnetic attractions are exact balances of electric current repulsions at every point in the electro-sphere of forces, and, as radial attractions are, within the sphere, measured by the mass of the ensphered body of the planet, it follows that the electro-sphere of forces around a gravital body hold it evenly balanced upon its pivotal center of revolution, and at the same time, to its path of motion around the sun.

When we gain such a conception of an electro-sphere of forces surrounding each revolving world, and of the grand potencies that these forces reveal in their joint combinations around a magnetic or gravital body, then the grand mysteries of planetary velocities will be solved, not as in the schools, by central forces, but by the grand flow of electric orbital forces from infinite sources of power in free space.

The machinery of the heavens is driven by power applied from the grand moving currents of virgin matter in space, as the ponderous water wheel is driven by currents of the waterfall applied to the periphery of the wheel, or perhaps as if an invisible power were applied to the rim of a ponderous balance wheel, depriving it of weight and imparting a grand velocity of motion from itself.

In such an electro-sphere of forces as I have here sketched we can readily detect the presence of that agency that gives circular waves around a stone cast into the water or around a disturbed center in the atmosphere, giving vibratory waves of sound, or waves of illumination around a burning body, or of heat moving out from a glowing fire through the atmosphere, while cold waves of air move toward the burning center.

We also learn from this electro-magnetic balance of the forces, that gravity in no case and in no place, either upon sun or planet, can become a crushing force hostile to organization or to the most delicate living form of being. I think that the specific gravity of the sun and planets demands a new system of weighing at the hands of the philosophers of the coming age.

In gathering up the thoughts suggested by this survey of the field of forces, under the command of electro-magnetic forces, we think we are justified in affirming:

1. That electricity reveals in its currents of energy, evidence of its commanding sovereignty over the sources of all power, and the material causes of all motion.

2. That the right angled force imparted to all planetary bodies in their path of motion is from space, and causative of the force of gravital attraction.

3. That all planetary motion is under the guidance of these companion forces, and that radial attraction and orbital repulsion are exact balances of each other at any point that may be taken, from the ponderable body of a planet to the extreme limits of its electro-sphere of forces.

4. The electro-sphere of forces holds the solid sphere of sun or planet on balanced centers within such electro-sphere, and magnetic or gravital relations between sun and planets is wholly determined by the mutually attracting combined forces of their electro-sphere.

Each body is weighed and nicely balanced by its own environed force currents, and hence the velocity of each planet in its own orbit of motion is determined by the closed circuits of orbital forces that flow around the central body around which it revolves.

5. In the grand electro-sphere of the sun the dead weight of the planets is eliminated from the problem of planetary motion and transferred to the problem of the forces, and the problem of the forces is solved in the nicely adjusted balances of the currents of force at every point in their fields of energy and motion.

The planets move in their orbits as freely and as silently as light in its grand streams of radiance. The velocity of the planets in their orbits is no more wonderful than the transmission of thought in symbols of impulse along our lines of telegraph.

In the field of the forces distances between magnetic centers of organic bodies of matter are reduced to insignificant measures. Impulses of energy pass between sun and earth in eight minutes of time by scientific measurements. This brings the two bodies into the closest sympathy. In fact, they both have their place in the same environment of forces, and are thrilled by the same pulses of sensation, and are bound each to each by the closest ties of likeness and reciprocal unity. As atoms fraternize with atoms, and currents of energy with currents of energy, so worlds sympathize with words, and in the closest bonds of unity keep each other company in their paths of motion.

By these same forces in lines of telegraphy, England and America signal each other as if in speaking distance, and by means of the telephone friends talk with friends hundreds of miles distant as if they were in their immediate presence.

CHAPTER IV.

GRAVITATION.

THE solar system is composed of revolving worlds which have taken on form and motion under the commanding presence of some natural potency that fixes their centers of revolution and orbits of motion, while it imparts to them a perpetual energy that gives to the entire system of worlds a perfection of order and harmony of velocities that proclaims their evolution out of the eternities past, and their perpetuity commensurate with the eternities to come. The power that upholds worlds and revolves them as the wheels of working machinery are revolved in the shop of the mechanic, must be eternal and infinite. It must have an all-pervading presence and uniform directing sovereignty over matter in all of its states and lines of motion, and must antedate matter in all organic forms and have been present with the light at the dawn of creation's first morning. As there could be no creative work till light appeared, so there could be no sun-systems of worlds before the flying spheres of organic matter took up their lines of curvelinear motion.

Such sovereign material potency is now recognized as the upholder and guide of satellites and planets in their varied revolutions and orbits of motion, as the power of gravitation. It has been assumed that this power is an emanation from organic bodies of matter that in some mysterious manner takes hold of other bodies of matter so as to attract each other mutually, with an intensity proportioned to the mass of such bodies directly, and as the squares of distance separating them inversely.

This assumption of rays of gravital influence going out as radial lines from one organic body of matter to another as an attracting medium between such bodies, has wrought constant confusion in the minds of scientific thinkers, and has given place to problems respecting light and gravity, that according to such assumption defy solution. The radiation of energy to accumulate energy in one body, that shall act as an attracting influence over other bodies, gives the absurd problem of the sun's radiation of light and heat to all planetary bodies, while he holds all such bodies to their orbits of motion by attractions that are as constant and enduring as the ages.

It is difficult to tell how the sun has gained his vast proportions and commanding influence over a system of revolving worlds while enveloped in an ocean of flame fed from the burning elements that have from some mysterious presence been fashioned into the sun's body preparatory to the kindling of the fires that are now burning for the convenience of a few satellites and planets.

Leaving these assumptions and problems of the schools respecting gravitation, I pass to notice the lines that gravital forces have fixed as a unified sovereignty over the sun and planetary bodies, giving them form and orbits of motion, constituting the solar system.

And first, the chosen lines of gravital forces are revealed in the spherical forms of sun and planets; and second, in their circular paths of motion.

The laws of motion impressed upon all bodies of matter are clearly revealed in their chosen centers of rest and curvelinear lines of motion. The great circles enclosing a sphere have all points that may be taken within them, a uniform distance from the center of the sphere, and the measure of one of the circles enclosing the sphere is the measure of all circles possible drawn around it. All right lines elementary to the construction of a sphere are radial lines drawn from the center of the sphere to points in the great circles in the perimeter of the sphere, and such radial lines extending indefinitely into space give the right lines of gravital impulse that all bodies of matter describe when let fall upon the earth. Now the astronomical measurements of gravital impulse are all determined upon radial lines joining the centers of two or more bodies in motion, and it has been discovered that such impulse is the same on all radial lines, disclosing a unity of pressure closing down around each world sphere, such pressure increasing toward the enclosed body according to gravital law.

Thus we find that the impulse or pressure of gravitation takes on the form of a sphere around each planetary body with its center the same as that of the enclosed body of organic spherical form; hence the impressing gravital sphere and the inclosed planetary sphere are bound together in a unity of form and pervaded by a unity of impulse. The same radial lines of central forces, and the same great circles of spherical boundaries are common to both the inclosed planetary body and the inclosing sphere of gravital forces. The inclosing gravital sphere is a material structure built out of vibrating lines of radial and right angled circular forces, that submits to the measuring line of distances and the computation of numbers as does the inclosed earthly structure of the planet, and must be exalted to its true place of sovereignty, *as matter*, over the suns and planetary bodies, that are revealed to the eye of the astronomer, before the perplexing problems of light, heat, world formation and planetary motion can find satisfactory solutions.

The sun's gravital sphere holds within its radial lines of restraining pressure, called attraction, bounded by the great circles of his spherical form, all the planetary bodies of the solar system with all of their varied paths of motion.

The sun's light pervades this entire gravital sphere reaching to Neptune, causing satellites and planets to evolve light and heat from their own environments of gravital pressure and velocities of revolution and motion as does the sun from the disturbance of gravital forces by the grand velocities of the planets in their orbits within his own gravital environing sphere.

Within the sun's gravital sphere there appears an association of planetary bodies, each having a separate identity with separate organic forms and individualized centers of rest and paths of motion; while each organic sphere must also be surrounded with its body of gravital impulse similar to that of the sun. Over this entire system of worlds, gravitation and light preside as co-working sovereignties, imparting from their material lines of energy to each planetary body of the solar system its individuality of form, strength and its power of illumination.

Once more let it be noticed that each gravital sphere of force-currents finds its measure in the organic body of matter in which its radial lines of force-currents find their center. Directly as mass and inversely as the squares of distance, gives the true law of measure for all gravital impulses. It is thus, because gravitation first builds from atomic centers to organic spherical bodies, and such bodies give the measuring unit of the impressing gravital spheres within which they are centrally bound. In other words the organic body of the planet is saturated by gravital energy to the full measure of its capacity to receive, from the radial lines of gravital pressure that converge upon the common gravital center of the inclosed and inclosing spheres.

The organic planetary body is as transparent to lines of gravital energy as the atmosphere is to rays of light. In fact, the organic matter that is built into the body of the planet is simply a materialization of gravital forces bound together and assorted into various substances by chemical affinities and held in place under converging lines of gravital pressure. As the life is superior to the form inclosing it so is the gravital material environment that incloses a planetary body and saturates it with energy superior to such body.

In making these assumptions I am not going a single line beyond the teaching of the schools. I recognize the same radial lines of gravital impulse—the same planetary spheres—the same great spherical boundaries of gravital impulse in which the planets take up their circular orbits of motion—the same mathematical problems that pertain to astronomical measurements and influence of sun and planets over each other in the grand harmonies of planetary motion; but where Sir Isaac Newton saw attraction of gravitation pulling an apple to the ground I think I see gravital pressure pushing it to the earth. Where he saw void space across which bodies attracted each other, I think I see well defined and perfectly constructed spheres of gravital and orbital force-currents of virgin matter closing down around each revolving world and filling inter-planetary space, through which they take up their paths of motion, bound each to each in bands of sympathy and mingling their rays of light and lines of an invisible gravital presence in a common solar unity.

Where Newton, looking back to a creative beginning, saw chaotic masses of matter either at rest or moving in straight lines, dead and inert, without power to set themselves in motion, and when set in motion having no power to stop; I think I see the companion material sovereignties of light and gravity compassing all space, holding all elements of matter in their lines of radiant energy, choosing centers of rest, and building world-spheres around such centers—building from themselves.

While the great philosopher found it necessary to invent the great problem of the parallelogram of forces to aid thought respecting Nature's methods of converting straight line motion under the dead force of inertia into orbital circles under the living gravital forces of attraction, I find no necessity for any such problem, for the material circles of gravital impulse are all mathematical circles, every possible radial line cutting them touches the circle at a uniform distance from the center of the circle, and all such points of contact give the conception of a mathematical point in motion at a uniform distance from the center of the circle around which it moves. There are no straight lines in either circles or spheres except radial lines. Straight lines cannot, even in imagination, give the conception of their construction into curved lines bounding the circle.

Finally, while the fall of an apple impressed the mind of Newton with the necessity of some occult force acting upon the apple pulling it to the earth, he was not impressed with the necessity of any such force in free space impelling the planets in their orbits across gravital attracting lines of force, each with a uniform velocity that finds no retarding influences in all the hitherto time periods of the ages.

Let the reader here note that while the lines are sharply drawn between the philosophy of our best scientific teachers and the philosophy of these papers, the writer cannot possibly detract from the deserved reputation of the old masters. The wonderful discoveries of the present age have led the way toward advanced positions of scientific thought, and the present papers are but little more than interpreters of such new discoveries.

If a new philosophy come into place discarding old errors, it must be an evolution from data furnished by the wonderful scientific discoveries of the present age. Old errors in physics must fade away in the light of new truths.

CHAPTER V.

GRAVITATION AND PLANETARY MOTION.

BY conceiving of organic matter and gravital forces as forming two concentric spheres, the former built from and by the latter and held centrally in its radial lines of force currents with an equal pressure upon, or along, each gravital line that can be let fall upon the organic body, we gain a standpoint of observation that will enable us to look with a clear vision into the sublimest wonders of creation's laboratory of material unfoldment.

But shall we leave at once the teachings of our schools that have been wrought into our intellectual being, impressing upon our minds the belief that gravital attracting forces going out from the sun in some mysterious manner, holding the planets to their circular orbits, are the sovereign cause of planetary motion? Shall we discard at once the thought that the worlds were made by an omnipotent hand, hurled into space in straight lines, and that the inertia of matter has kept them circling around central suns, keeping time for the ages?

Had we dared to part company with these thoughts in our childhood it would have banished some childish fears lest inertia should grow tired and our earth would fall into the sun and be burned up, like scientific meteors, to light and heat other worlds.

It is the deisre of the writer that the reader will stand

firmly by the old theories of attraction of gravitation until he is able to reverse thought in the study of the problem,

That, *Gravitation centralizes energy in the creation, or evolution, of matter in organic forms, that as units, they may hold their place and act their part in the grand groupings of a universal creative unity.*

I care not how narrow or how broad the field of vision brought under the eye of the thoughtful pupil, the problem will afford its own solution. The mustard seed and the acorn are fashioned by the same forces that build world spheres, and the plumb lines of gravity hold all created objects in place, and give to all objects a distinct personality and a living environment.

I introduce these thoughts that we may gain conceptions of gravitation from our own field of measures and experiences. The astronomer with his telescope directed to Jupiter, and his eye on the glass, observing his phenomena, finds lines of gravity holding intercourse between the great sphere of the planet and the little eyeball of the philosopher.

But it is earth gravity that saturates the eye to its completeness of pressure that gives to all eyeballs the sense of vision. The gravital spheres of earth and Jupiter thrill with responsive sensations, each to each, and such sensations are imparted to each organic body within the organic forms of their respective planetary bodies, while through the varied material organisms composing the bodily structures of the two planets, each atom within them is reached by gravital sensory impulses. Individuality of form and identity of being are creations under the centralizing touch of gravital forces, grouping sensitive atoms into various substances, and such substances into the infinitesimal forms of organic matter, and the infinitely varied forms of vegetable and animal life. Thus the great, universal and all pervading forces of gravity become a material providence over every individuality of form and being, and as gravital impulse is instantaneous in its action and reaction between bodies of matter, rest and motion, among gravitally bound bodies in the solar system, may be cancelled from the problem of planetary changes. The bodies are actually at rest while relatively in motion.

Gravitation makes no record of distances. It gives fixed centers of rest to all planetary bodies in free space, and binds body to body by mutual central reactions between them, thus annihilating distance within the solar system, grouping all planetary bodies within the system in one gravital sphere of unified force currents having the center of the sun the center of the sphere, while responsive impulses of gravity within the solar sphere all blend in harmonious unity, rest, silence, cold and darkness dominating over all. The planets, with their satellites, fulfill their time periods of revolution with mathematical accuracy, under the action and reaction of gravital force currents, insomuch that seconds are not lost or time hastened in the great circles of the ages.

Strange that scientific teachers should talk of burned out suns or wrecked and dying worlds! Strange that such order should come out of grand world burnings; or that scientific prophets should teach the childish stories of central fires either in sun or planets.

Before we can reach correct conclusions respecting the relations existing between gravital impulse and planetary motion, certain fundamental truths respecting the nature and methods of gravitation as a creative and moving energy operating through and around matter, should be clearly fixed in the mind.

1. The source of gravital energy is free space. Wherever worlds appear, there gravitation finds its home and reveals its presence in the fashioning, upholding, enlightening and revolving them. Not a point can be fixed in space where gravital energy is not; hence it is not transferable from place to place because its control of matter in bodily form is complete and commanding. The center of all organic bodies of matter are gravital centers, while rest or motion is under the control of gravital currents of force. Gravity comes from no whither, and goes to no whence. No ether of the scientist can either help it or hinder it in its work.

2. The energy of gravitation is the energy of elemental atoms of matter that take on the forms of linear vibrating currents of force, and thus pervade both matter and space.

3. The central lines of force-currents that represent radial lines of pressure in all gravitally charged bodies, are complemented by lateral or right angled lines of pressure that become currents of impulse of equal lateral strength or tensity to the radial lines of impulse, at equal distances from the fixed gravital center of the body; hence the formation of spherical bodies of matter under the impress of gravital forces, and the circular paths of motion of the planets within the sun's gravital sphere of forces.

These orbital, or right-angled currents of force are as fixed and definite in their currents of impulse around the sun and his planets, respectively, as are the radial lines of currents that become plumb lines of pressure upon such bodies. The pressure toward and around the central sun is the same at every point in the planet's orbit of motion.

4. Transmission of pressure or impulse between the sun and his planets is not by means of the interference of currents of force between the various bodies, but each body becomes a unit of aggregated impulses, centrally bound and centrally unified, and hence their influence is confined to a single radial line joining the respective centers of the solar system in a social compact of revolving worlds; each world commanding its own field of impulses of gravital energy, and each world evolving its own light, heat, moisture and life from the environing field where they appear. In short, gravital forces can not do work where they are not, and consequently at any point taken within a gravital sphere the pressure is equal to the mathematical measuring lines of such gravital sphere. The pressure at the surface of the earth at sea level is the same at all points that may be taken on the earth, and on all plumb-lines extending outward from such points the pressure is the same at equal distances from the earth. This gives us the law of gravital pressure, which is directly as mass and inversely as the cube of distance—not "square of distance," as taught in the schools—for, spheres are to each other as the cubes of their radii.

By consulting this law we find that the earth's mass is an exact measure of the pressure of the gravital field of

GRAVITATION AND PLANETARY MOTION.   73

forces environing it, and such environing field decreases in pressure as distances and radial lines from the body increase, until the environing sphere gives pressure upon the earth equal to the gravity or weight of the earth's mass.

Fix these thoughts in mind and then it will be seen that each body of the solar system is upheld and balanced in space upon and from its own gravital center.

When this standpoint of thought is gained, and we refer to the orbits of the planets, and find that the area of each orbit is fixed by a radial line joining the center of the planet to the center of the sun, and that the velocity of the planet is so evenly balanced as to time periods, that its radial line joining the two bodies, moves over equal areas in equal time-periods; then it follows that the velocity of the planet in its orbit is an even balance at each point in its orbit of motion of the unit of pressure of the sun's radial line of pressure toward his own gravital center.

This velocity is the centrifugal force of the schools and is at each point of motion a tendency of the planet to fly outward from its orbit, such tendency having been ascribed to the inertia of the matter composing the body of the planet.

It may aid thought if we vary our methods of dealing with the problem of the forces that constitute the gravital sphere of forces, to call lines of radial pressure, lines of magnetic condensation and lines of orbital pressure, lines of diffusion, and the two forces that these radial and orbital lines represent as balancing forces at any point in a sphere of forces that may be taken.

Radial central forces give aggregating centers of rest,

6

while orbital forces of diffusion give the carrying lines of the forces in free space.

In the charge of these forces, atomic forms of matter divide themselves, giving rest and motion, building matter into organic forms and balancing worlds in motion as evenly as the lines of light are balanced between sun and earth.

In the charge of these balancing forces there is no rest without motion, and no motion without rest. Darkness and light, cold and heat, growth and decay, organic forms of matter having life and enfolding life-germs, and life-germs unfolding into life-forms, are all dependent upon the action and reaction of these jointly working forces.

With this seeming digression that we have introduced for the purpose of better acquainting the reader with the true cause of the centrifugal forces of planetary motion, we would refer to the actual velocity of the planets in their orbits of motion around the sun, in confirmation of the outward pressure of curvelinear or orbital currents of force acting over against central radial currents of pressure, constituting the closed orbits of the planets in their order of motion around the sun.

It is clearly evident that the velocity of each planet in its orbit indicates the measure of pressure acting upon the body to drive it outward from the body of the sun into space.

Now, by referring to the table of planetary velocities, we find Mercury, the planet nearest the sun, has a velocity of 105,330 miles per hour. Venus, the next in order, moves at the rate of 77,050 miles per hour, while our earth only travels at the rate of 65,533 miles per hour. Thus the velocities of the planets in their orbits continue to decrease as their distances from the sun increase until Neptune, the outmost planet from the sun, has a velocity of only 11,968 miles. Thus as gravital pressure toward the sun is greatest at the sun's body and decreases as the squares of distance outward increase, so does the centrifugal pressure of each planet in the series decrease, causing each planet to move in a closed orbit, and in fixed time periods.

The mean velocity of each planet in its orbit continues the same, age after age, because it is held in the constant charge of central pressure toward the sun, and outward pressure into free space. The central pressure of force currents upon a planet in its orbit make it a unit of force, and fix its center of revolution, while the outward pressure of the circular currents of force cause the planet to revolve on its axis. These radial and orbital currents of force constitute the gravital sphere that holds each revolving world in charge, and from which all power in matter giving rest and motion, is derived.

These companion forces individualize the sun and the planetary bodies of his system of worlds and also group them in one comprehensive gravital sphere of reciprocal sympathy and perpetual harmony.

Each planet of the solar system acts upon each one of the family of planets and also upon the central sun as a unit, and the central radial line extending from center to center of the influencing bodies is the measure of the unit of influence that they reciprocally exert over each other. Confining the thought to the gravital ties that bind earth to sun and sun to earth, it will be noticed that along the radial line joining the center of the sun to the center of the earth there is fixed the center of the earth's hemisphere of light and heat. This line always marks the culminating point of the sun's illuminating power upon the earth. Where this point touches the earth there is the noon of an unending day. The unit of the earth's revolution measures the unit of light and heat that the earth receives from the sun, and the unit of the earth's motion in her orbit during a single revolution, gives the unit of the earth's area of daily motion in her orbit around the sun; with this radial line of the earth's orbit a constant measure of the earth's gravital ties binding her to the central sun, giving the closed orbit, that gives the unit of years that fixes the measuring line of the eternities, both past and to come.

That sun and earth should thus be bound to each other by reciprocal units of influence, measured by the coinciding radial lines of the sun and earth; and that these coinciding lines should give the uniform distance of the earth from the sun in its orbit, must be accounted for as a grand factor in the problem of gravital potencies. There must be a grand working unity of gravital force currents to give units of work. We note the units of work in the uniformity of light and the time periods of the earth's revolution; we know that the area of the earth's motion in her orbit is measured in time periods, by the area passed over by this line joined as it is at all times to the center of the earth, touching as it does the center of the earth and the line of the earth's orbit of motion, and, also, the center of the sun at the center of the orbit; but we do not seem to know, except in a general way, referring all to attraction of gravitation, how the work is done. But at the earth's distance from the sun there is a unit expression of two lines of force acting in harmony, and yet one acting over against the other. A unit of attraction pulls the earth toward the sun, while a unit of repulsion carries the earth at right angles to central attractions with a repelling force equal to such attractions.

We have endeavored in these papers to note the working unity of these two forces in all displays of gravital or electro-magnetic energy.

By referring to the chapter on magnetism it will be seen that the magnet reveals power in the combination of radial attracting currents of force with repellant currents of force crossing the magnet at right angles. A passing current of electricity will compel a magnetic needle to take up its position at right angles to the passing current. In a magnet the electric currents moving around it must be of equal strength to its power of attraction; extending outward from the central line of the magnet, creating a magnetic field unified and complete from pole to pole of the magnet.

The unit of power or force of such magnet is chiefly revealed at the poles, and at such poles is of equal strength. Such magnets only serve as a connecting couple between electrified bodies of matter when they are of opposite electrical states. Like poles repel each other, while unlike attract. Now we have in mind the central tie binding each planet to the center of the central sun; and the forces that preside over planetary motion find their unit of work always submitting to this measuring line of the planets' area of motion in its orbit, and also fixing its time periods of revolution that give the working days of creation and the circling years of the eternities of perpetual continuance.

Thus the problems of light, heat, gravity and planetary revolution must find their solution in the enfolded potencies of this radius-vector of astronomical science. It is the base line of all astronomical measurements, both of distance and magnitude; even planetary velocities find their limits of measure in the units of potency that remain constant grouped around this flying radial line of each planet's orbit of motion. The action and reaction of the sun's gravital influence over the planets find their complete expression at the terminal points of the radius-vector. In like manner the radial gravital pressure of each body is centered upon the same terminal points.

Now we have already regarded the forces of gravitation as the centralizing and orbital currents of force of an electro-magnetic field of forces in spherical form centered at the center of the organic body. We now have to consider the behavior of gravitally charged bodies over each other within a common gravital field of forces. The radius-vector, then, seems to unify the gravital energy that holds the two worlds in charge. The unit of influence of sun and earth over each other, gives the unit of energy that at every mathematical point along this radius-vector is constant. This is the normal line of magnetization joining center to center of the magnetic or gravital fields of the two influencing bodies; such line having position, but neither magnitude nor rest. It is simply the constant expression of the magneto-electric energy of a constant field of force currents. The two world spheres at its terminals are vast magnets with their magnetic fields intersphereing each other. If one accept the teachings of science this line represents the reciprocal gravital attraction of the bodies over each other, consequently the sun terminal of the line expresses the attraction of the sun upon the earth, while the earth terminal represents the attraction of the earth upon the sun.

These terminals are, then, similar to the poles or terminals of a bar magnet. They are of equal potential and are immersed in fields of equal potentials; we consequently conclude that the radius-vector of a planet's orbit has its magnetic field of force currents revolving around it giving it both position and power with the position of rest and motion that polar forces give to the axial line joining them in each magnetically charged planetary body. Thus the radius-vector becomes the axial line of a field of gravital energy having a magnetic field of force currents grouped around it as real as those grouped around the organic spheres of earth and sun. This gravital field of the radius-vector constitutes a field of spherical forces that is an exact measure of the reciprocal influences that sun and earth exert over each other. It has its line of rest in the great plane of the ecliptic. Its measures of attraction between the two bodies fix the orbital line of the earth's distance from the sun, and its area of motion is an exact measure of the sun's repellent field of energy exerted upon the earth within her orbit of motion. In short, the unit of influence that the sun and earth exert over each other is grouped around the flying line of the radius-vector as gravital forces are grouped around the organic bodies of sun and earth. This intervening grouping of a gravital organism of force currents between sun and earth around a central line joining the center of the two bodies, simplifies the problem of gravital potencies, and renders clear to intellectual vision the restful states of organic bodies, while in their relations to each other they take up velocities in fixed paths of motion that transcend all sensible measures.

Like a magnet this intervening central line joining the centers of sun and planets, finds its energy of attraction or pressure greatest at its terminals or poles at the rest centers of the two gravitally bound bodies, and diminishing outward from such center still the rest center of the intervening field of gravital forces is reached. Thus the centers of the two world spheres are at rest, and held at rest by a unit of pressure or attraction that remains constant. So at each point in the line of central binding the attraction is constant and restful, only measured by distance from the influencing planetary body. The intervening field of forces has a fixed center of rest at equal distances from sun and earth, and groups the gravital forces between the two spheres in a gravital sphere of unit strength as real and enduring as the gravital spheres that hold sun and earth in charge. This sphere of organic force currents is constantly changing from radial line to radial line of the

GRAVITATION AND PLANETARY MOTION. 81

earth's orbit, as its axial line of energy, while its field of organic force currents remains constant through the constantly acting inductive influence of sun and earth upon each other. The forces centered in sun, earth and radius-vector, remain constant because the field of the forces through which the planets move is a uniform field of current energy, while each rest center gives unity to the field of forces that environ it, and seeming rest to all planetary bodies in their orbits of motion. Each planetary body is held at rest in its field of unified currents of force, while the forces that environ it take on the velocity of the light and hold all gravitally charged bodies so nicely balanced on their centers of revolution that the rocky foundations of suns and planets are built securely around them.

If any student of physical phenomena questions the solution of the problem of planetary motion here given let such a one experiment with magnets and currents of electricity and mark their behavior in a common field and it will appear that they always combine their strength by flowing at right angles to each other. Currents of electricity flowing around a bar of soft iron induce magnetism in the iron, revealing its attracting energy at the terminals of the bar.

Neither magnetic attractions nor electrical repulsions are revealed except in these natural bindings each to each around a common center. Separate from each other they do no work, hence those forces must thus have their combination around the radius-vector to make it the unit measure of gravital attraction between sun and earth.

The old ideas of lines of light, or lines of gravity, of

more than ninety-two millions of miles in length passing from body to body conveying light and gravital energy, must be abandoned. The presence of such ideas in the mind of the writer will find expression in the pages of this work resulting from old conceptions of light and gravity, and it is a seeming necessity that we adhere to old methods of thought in the revelation of new truths. It is in the infinite divisibility of light, suited to the infinity of objects that are touched by its radiance, that we must look for correct conceptions of its linear structure.

The eye takes in light as a unit of expression with its central line of sensation, as the earth takes it in with her central line joining the center of earth and sun, giving it a constant noonday measure of light. As the gravital or magnetic strength of the earth is the measure of its unit of light and heat from the sun, so is the eye the measure of the light and heat taken in from the sun, giving the sensation of vision.

The transmission of the energy of light and gravity from sun to earth and earth to sun thus becomes a mere balance of forces maintained between the two bodies by the magnetic strength of the central line joining them to each other as magnets. The smaller magnetic body becomes the measure of magnetic strength, or illumination it will receive.

The same law of intercommunion exists between all organic bodies as to their reception of gravity or light. Such bodies do not receive rays of light or gravity by impact, but from internal sensory disturbances of light forces and gravital forces centered within them. The lines of light passing through the lens of the eye only give the sensation of light by touching the center of magnetic sensation within the body insomuch that the entire being takes in the impulse and is thrilled with the sensation.

Thus the energy of light, heat and gravity is weighed or measured in the electro-magnetic balances of sensation within the influenced organism and from the environing field in which the body finds place. The flying spheres of the solar system, the localized spheres of animal vision, and the sun-fashioned spheres of the mustard seed of the garden, are alike recipients of the universal energy of light, heat and gravity, in their individual fields of universal rest and motion, while they influence each other along the central line of impulse joining their respective centers. Thus infinites of individualities are bound in one universal unity. Each individuality has its fixed center of rest in its uniform field of sustaining and governing potencies; and each takes in light and gravity by unit of sensation measured by its unit of form.

The transference of sensation across many miles of distance through magnetic conduction, as witnessed in the phenomena of the telephone, is a seeming mystery, and yet the connecting wire that takes up the vibrations of sound at one terminal of the wire, repeating them accurately to the ear at the other terminal, involves the same mystery that is involved in the transference of sensations of light from sun to earth and earth to sun along the gravital line of the radius-vector. The entire mystery of such transference of sensations is enfolded in the mysterious working forces of the magnet. The magnet reveals its unit of current vibrations, constituting its entire working energy, alike at each pole. The entire combination of force currents that give to the magnet its strength, reveal that strength in equal polar vibrations that are responsive to each other, each to each, giving duplicate expressions of all disturbing sensations at either pole.

Bear in mind that light, heat, gravitation, magnetism and electricity, are simply vibrating expressions of the same lines of force currents, and hence the magnetically charged wire of the telephone, also the gravitally charged line of the radius-vector speak and evolve light with a unit of expression, at the same unit of time at either pole of their unit of centrally bound forces. Thus the vibrations of light at the terminal of the radius-vector on the sun, are the same on the earth, and thus sun light and earth light impart the same sensations to the inhabitants of their respective spheres.

The intense activity of the polar forces of the radius-vector on earth and sun is resisted by the non-conducting atmosphere of their magnetically charged bodies evolving light and heat on the hemispheres of the two bodies looking towards each other, while the organic structures of sun and earth are correspondingly thrilled by disturbed electro-magnetic impulses equal to revolving and warming them, and thereby imparting to the circulating currents of their solid spheres such activities as promote crystalization of the rocks, evolution of the oils and gases, with the streams of water that permeate earth-formations, as circulating life currents permeate the animal and vegetable structures that are built upon the earth.

The same forces that give the light and heat of the sun upon the earth are also warming and creating forces within the earth. The revolution of the planets and the evolution of life and form within and upon the earth and sun, are simply diverse expressions of the all-pervading material potencies that give strength to the magnet.

If these statements are accepted, it follows that all earth disturbances must be referred to the working presence of electro-magnetic forces.

Storms, earthquakes and volcanoes come into place by non-conducting forms of matter in some way resisting the flow of currents of electric energy between heavily charged bodies of matter of opposite potentials. Light, heat and explosive vibrations of currents giving sound, reveal the pathways of electro-magnetic forces.

CHAPTER VI.

EVOLUTION OF LIGHT.

GRAVITATION, magnetism and electricity have hitherto been but little more than names for mysterious dynamic potencies. Had the ancients been made acquainted with their works of marvelous power and varied possibilities, as we now observe them, temples and altars would have been erected for them, and they would have been regarded as chief among the gods. In fact the darkness and the light are both alike unto them. From everlasting to everlasting they are the same. Their lines have gone out into all worlds and they hold in their charge all of the orderings of a material providence over everything that has form or motion in all of the infinites of worlds.

The forces they represent, are, in Nature invisible, and do their normal work in cold and darkness. They are not generated forces, but on the contrary are generating forces. They are not dependent forces, neither are they secondary, but elementary, both as matter and force. We now know that electricity and magnetism evolve light and heat, but as to gravitation our teachers are all silent. On the contrary, they teach that while gravitation holds the planets to the sun in their various orbits of motion, that the burning body of the sun sends out to such planets on radial lines all the light and heat that they share. In short, that the central sun commanding the revolutions and orbital velocities of his family of worlds, is constantly consumed by raging fires of the intensest heat, that they may be warmed and illuminated; and still our cities with their shops and dwellings are now lighted from the cold, dark currents of electrical and magnetic impulse.

Respecting the devices for evolving and handling the electro-magnetic currents that feed the electric flame, I need only say here that they serve to intensify electric currents in their conducting wires, and such currents further intensified at the points of illumination by forcing their way through non-conducting mediums.

The dynamo machines are accumulators of electric energy that evolves light at broken points in the conducting wires, or where non-conducting substances are interposed in the circuits, that intensify the power of the currents at the broken terminals of the conducting wires where light and heat are revealed.

These devices, in short, accumulate insensible and dark currents of force in conducting wires from which light and heat are evolved at resisting breaks in their circuits of motion. The light and heat thus evolved are fed from the flowing currents and fall upon objects of vision giving the sensations of illumination within a hemisphere of radiating impulses similar to the rays of light that go forth from burning bodies of matter.

Now let the student of physical phenomena place the electric light in the same field with the flame-bearing compounds that illuminate our dwellings, and notice the intimate fellowship existing between the cold, dark forces of electricity and magnetism, and light and heat, as the sovereign radiating forces of material energy.

The electric light and the light of a candle are essentially the same while the sources from which they derive their power of illumination seem radically different. The former feeds upon resisted and broken currents of invisible forces, while the latter feeds upon visible bodies of organic matter.

But the candle has a history back of itself. If it came from the fat of animals, they fed upon vegetation that came into place under the play of sun forces and earth forces. From these they received life, light and heat, and took on form, that in the flame of illumination is passing back again to the field of forces whence they came.

All organic bodies of matter that are consumed in the heat and light of illumination, or under the wasting process of oxidation, are in a transition state from the forces that evolve light and life to their primal home in the same forces, thus giving the completed circuits of life and death, of creation and destruction. The world's immortality is complete in these closed circuits of transformation that have no beginning and no end.

The data here given lead us to an acquaintance with light and heat as evolved radiating currents of force, flashing out from local centers where powerful resistants intercept the flow of cumulative and intensified electric currents breaking up their unity of construction and diffusing their energy on radiating lines glowing with intensified electro-magnetic impulses—such impulses always unified from the disturbed centers of emanation.

The electric light and the electric illumination of the storm-cloud only differ from each other in their time periods of continuance; the former is fed from a constant current of uniform flow, intercepted by constant resistance, evolving therefrom a constant illumination, while the latter is the transference of electric energy at high tension from one cloud to another, or from cloud to earth through the non-conducting atmosphere, at a single impulse.

It should be constantly borne in mind, that in all cases of electrical disturbance evoking sensible displays of power, the normal balance of the forces is broken by some resisting agency, while the work done by the forces to overcome such disturbance is simply a forcible readjustment of such balances. The terms positive and negative, and the algebraic signs plus and minus are used by the electrician to denote the two different electrical conditions of bodies of matter assumed under frictional excitement. When electricity is produced by friction it is found invariably, that equal quantities of positive and negative electricity are produced.

The normal flow of the positive and negative currents of electricity is in equally balanced quantities, moving in opposite directions. Thus flowing, they bind themselves to bodies of matter in units of strength, each body of matter thus bound having its center fixed by the centralizing dynamic energy of electro-magnetic balancing forces. This leads us to the consideration of the same concentric spheres under the working presence of electro-magnetic potencies that we have considered under the dynamic pressure of gravital forces. Each planetary body is not only a magnet but an electro-magnet. The organic matter of the body of the planet, that our old philosophers have called "brute matter" is as passive in the embrace of gravital and orbital currents of force as is the soft iron core of the electro-magnet in the circling currents of electricity that pass through the coil of insulated wire that encircles it.

The strength of the electro-magnet comes and goes at the touch of the electrician who presses the keys, that make and break the circuit conveying energy from battery to magnet. The pressure that holds the keeper to the magnet is solely under the command of the encircling currents of energy that flow around it, and such currents can only be brought under the charge of the electrician by mechanical disturbance of the dark and insensible forces of the magnetically or gravitally charged earth.

To make clear our philosophy of thought respecting the combination and division of the forces of the electromagnet, that we regard as synonymous with gravital forces, including both radial and orbital forces; it must be noted that we are here contemplating matter in two equally balanced states, which we would denominate fixed matter and free matter, the former organic and magnetic, the latter linear and electric.

These two states of matter are inseparable from each other and in all of their combinations of creative work they fix centers of aggregation and formulate concentric spheres of magnetization and electrization around such centers.

In the combination of these two states of matter the

organic becomes restful and abiding under the pressure of radial magnetizing forces, while it at the same time finds its rest in the charge of the commanding carrying forces that constitute the great electrosphere of forces of linear matter in space.

This electrosphere of linear vibrating force-currents is self-sustained and self-fashioned out of currents of elementary matter as real as the rivers. The balance of the electro-magnetic current, inwrought into spherical forms is so complete that, though their velocity is as the light, they become restful as the ocean, and as abiding as the ages in their normal combinations of form and lines of work. Lines of gravity are the same at every point that may be taken upon the surface of the earth, and at any point that may be taken between earth and sun the gravital measure of strength has not changed since sun and earth were built. The light that seems to go and come evening and morning has continued to shed its benign influence through the hemisphere looking toward the sun from the period of the earth's first revolution to the present time. Earth-light is a perpetual flame; it never ceases to burn and yet it is a constant evolution from earth currents and sun currents. It is fed from material elements as truly as the lights in our dwellings.

In confirmation of these statements we have only to refer to the devices now used for giving artificial supplies of both water and light to the inhabitants of our principal cities. The city of Chicago is built by the side of a vast fountain of pure water that is held securely within its banks by gravital pressure. To bring water from the lake in flowing currents to the dwellings and along the streets of the city water is lifted by the repulsive power of steam driving vast engines, forcing it through conducting pipes to an elevated artificial reservoir from which it flows freely by gravital pressure, through all the water mains of the city to all of its inhabitants. Chicago is also built upon a vast sea of light giving currents of energy; such energy is held at rest under the grand centralizing forces of gravity. This vast sea of forces when disturbed by the sun's presence in the heavens evolves a light sufficient to enlighten all of the inhabitants of one hemisphere of the earth. The revolution of the earth and sun, working over against each other, resisted by the atmospheric envelope of the two rapidly revolving spheres, lift the sea of dark forces that are at the feet of their inhabitants up to the high temperature of the noon of day, under the controlling presence of the noonday's sun, causing the dark forces to burst into a sea of flame, warming and enlightening all of the peoples of the earth alike, during a single revolution of the earth.

This is Nature's method of both lighting and watering the earth; for the fountains of waters that are formed above the earth, giving clouds and centralized storms with their winds and rain, are lifted to their place by the same disturbing forces of sun and earth that give light and heat. But what of the night? The city of Chicago needs night illumination as truly as she needs flowing currents of water. She calls to her aid the electrician and he makes his plant of powerful engines and systems of conducting wires, and builds his high towers, or seeks elevated points to which he can lead off his powerful currents of force from his dynamo machines driven by huge balance wheels that are set in motion by the repellant power of steam. But when all these preparations are completed there is everything necessary for lighting the city except the light. Where is the fountain to be drawn upon to feed the lamps that are placed at the resisting breaks in the conducting wires, at the chosen points of illumination? I answer, It is the same fountain of force currents that is drawn upon by the sun, to evolve the light of day. It is at the feet of every dweller upon the earth. It is centered in every eye that takes in vision from the light, and in every seed-germ that takes on life. Its sea level of darkness and rest is the same as that of the ocean; and it must be disturbed in its place of rest in the darkness and lifted forcibly through the conducting wires leading to its fixed points of illumination before it assumes its garments of light that are ample for the envelopment of the city. The light thus produced is self-evolved, self-lighted, having a fountain as exhaustless as space is immeasureable. The currents of force that feed the electric light are as truly matter, as the currents of water flowing through the water pipes of the city, fed from the elevated reservoirs of supply that are constantly replenished by the working energy of the huge pumping engines at the border of the lake. It seems strange that while our cities are abandoning candle and lamp, petroleum and gas, for the electric light, that science should continue to teach that the creator of worlds kindled an intensely devouring flame upon the surface of the sun to light the planets millions of miles distant in the cold and dark regions of space.

CHAPTER VII.

HEAT, LIGHT AND LIFE EVOLVED FROM DISTURBED ELECTRO-MAGNETIC FORCES OF ENVIRONMENT.

HEAT, light and life are joint evolutions from material conditions of organic matter, also from centers of resistance in currents of the electric forces, under high tension from conduction.

I say joint evolutions because of their joint dependence upon interior work performed in matter, to secure material conditions that report to the senses as heat, light and life.

Prof. Tyndall has prepared an exhaustive treatment of the theme " Heat as a mode of motion" in which he seems to regard heat as an index, denoting the transference of energy through bodies of matter, doing work in overcoming the resistance of bodies held under the energy of attraction, which he styles potential energy, to the extreme of repulsion, which he styles dynamic energy.

Heat, then, is an expression of energy in motion from attraction to repulsion, or, in other words, it is the language of the working energy of repulsion in bodies of matter overcoming the attraction that gives them organic or bodily form. But there is another language of transference of energy by means of light and heat, from the dynamic energy of light and heat of environing space to the organic growths of material structures. The latter is the working energy of creative forces, and the sustaining energy of heat in doing that interior work in bodies that is a constant support of unfolding life forms.

With reference to this transference of energy he says, "As potential energy disappears, dynamic energy comes into play. *Throughout the universe the sum of these two energies is constant.*"

We have, then, to simply note the two extreme points noted by the arc of motion of these two energies, to discover the whence of matter and force in repulsion. Heat light and life, in creation of bodily forms bring matter from its radiant state at the low level of the cold and the darkness of free space to its rest in organic structures under the energy of attraction, and through an inverse order of work under the repelling energy of heat and light it passes back to its home in space. Thus, light, heat and life are the paths of the dynamic conditions of matter coming under the power of potential energy in body, and also by a reversed order of work, heat, light and extinction of life, indicate the return of matter to its native radiant condition in space.

The active work of these two grand energies of the universe is thus revealed upon the elevated plane of light and heat; commencing and ending at the low level of the cold and the darkness.

The great mystery of the problem is hidden with the silent work of these two energies, doing work in their elementary lines of force in the dark and cold floods of universal gravity that compass space, in which they guide and revolve the sun systems of worlds, which are the expression of the modes of motion of matter in charge of the same two energies of attraction and repulsion that evolve light, heat and life. The dynamic of gravital forces compasses all conditions of matter and all modes of motion. Cold and darkness, heat and light, in their greatest possible intensity give the limits of attraction and repulsion, and all of matter has its change of states, and its lines of motion, between these natural limits. The dynamic of cold is attraction, while the dynamic of heat is repulsion; the former are centralizing forces, the latter are carrying orbital forces; bodies of matter come to rest atom by atom, under charge of centralizing currents of force, while they are revolved in their orbits of motion on repellent currents of force. Centralizing dynamic energy is hidden under the dynamic states of matter in body, while orbital dynamic energy is hidden within the great cold depths of virgin matter moving freely in space; but these two classes of energy are companion forces bound each to each so that "the sum of these two energies is constant" and reciprocal, always conditioned by central bindings of matter in organic conditions.

These two energies compass the universality of energy, filling all space, and holding in charge every atom of free matter, and every organic body of matter in all suns and sun systems that fill immensity; while they at the same time become infinitely divisible, suited to the individualizing of all organizing or evolving bodies of matter whether crystalline, or organic having life. These two classes of energy individualize themselves, imparting to each individuality an entirety of likeness that belongs to seed-germ and fruitage, in all the myriad lines of paternity and sonship that are unfolded to philosophic experiment or to theological conceptions. Thus the image of the Creator is seen in the eternal sonship of all things that take on form, and in all forms having life. The division of these two classes of energy into potential and dynamic only gives sensible measures to the unseen and the immeasureable. Neither of them becomes potential. They are both dynamic; permeating matter as freely as they compass space, always respecting the measures of aggregating centers, while they are both interblended and evenly balanced in all their displays of power, or in their modes of motion. Strictly speaking, bodies of matter do not attract directly as mass and inversely as square of distance; but the dynamic forces of matter move to, through and around bodies of matter with a united strength conditioned by matter in body and distance;—intensity of central attractions over orbital repulsions, varying inversely as the squares of distance.

With this conception of the two grand energies of attraction and repulsion woven into each other's embrace, in radial and orbital impulses constituting a spherical network of orbital and radial currents of force, flowing around and toward each revolving world, it is not difficult to see how sun and planets are grouped in one sympathetic family grouping, of revolving spheres, under the charge of purely dynamic conditioning forces.

Potential energy is thus eliminated from the great problem of gravital forces, and space, cold, dark and silent, appears as grouped around world centers in ever-flowing linear streams of energy, that are the perennial source of virgin matter and planetary motion.

Thus the two grand energies of space carry the great spheres so evenly poised upon the electro magnetic floods of attraction and repulsion, that all planetary motion is without resistance. Sensible forms of matter are as the commanding presence of the dynamic forces that fashioned them, and have constant care of their organic unity.

Thus it will appear that elements of matter are elements of the force currents that localize bodies of matter and preside over their modes of motion. These elements are in currents, electro dynamic and repellent, and magneto-dynamic and attractive. They constitute the balancing units of universal energy and conserve all displays of power in universal harmony. Their home is in the cold, silent darkness of universal space, In them heat, light and life find the sources of their power and the elementary lines of their visible continuance. Heat, light and life come into place through local disturbances, or local resistants to the harmony of these currents of dynamic energy. Out of these currents the cold flint and steel bring light. From them the rubbed sticks of the savage derives a fire that warms him and cooks his food. The scientist by friction upon the revolving disk of his electric machine gathers powerful electrical divided currents and performs experiments in electricity and magnetism, and he finds light and heat springing forth from the disturbed currents that proclaim the whence of their power and the what of their illumination.

HEAT, LIGHT AND LIFE. 99

The oxidizing of metals in the battery gives electrical currents, that, interrupted in their paths of metallic conduction, give light and heat. Even the rubbed ice of the scientist disturbs the flow of these currents to such a degree as to evolve heat. *They are then latent heat, latent light, and latent sources of life and also latent chords of sound.*

As to the transmission of light and heat we regard them as always obeying the laws ot magnetic and electrical conduction and as, in fact, simply disturbed and illuminated electro-magnetic currents of force revealing heat and light where mechanical disturbance intercepts and breaks up their normal lines of conduction. The lines of radial and orbital currents surrounding and permeating every magnetic body are the great carrying lines of sensation and hence light to the eye, sound to the ear, heat to the body, taste to the tongue and flavor to the nostrils are conveyed in the vibratory currents of electro-magnetic impulse. Heat and light are evolved from the environment of their field of illumination and influence. The light of the sun is confined to his own sphere of radiance, so is the light of the earth evolved at the base of its incumbent atmosphere where gravital sun currents and earth currents meet under the disturbance of the non-conducting atmosphere.

The electrician carries no lighted lamp from his dynamo machines of propagation to his centers of illumination. He feeds the brilliant flames of his electric lamps with the dark streams of electrical impulse through conducting wires that convey energy but not light. It is thus that the closed circuits of magneto-electrical impulses between sun and earth and earth and sun convey energy from body to body in reciprocal counterflowing currents that furnish a constant illumination upon both earth and sun—each body receiving light and heat in exact proportion to the strength of their respective sources of magnetic energy affording as they do, gravital connections and battery impulses, sufficient for a perpetual evolution of both earth-light and sunlight.

It should be here stated that light and heat are evolved from gravital attractions whether upon sun or earth, and that the light and heat of *radiating* centers are from centers of *combustion*, and hence local and temporary. They cut no figure in the great problem of world illumination.

The sun radiates heat and light to the limits of his illuminated atmosphere and here radiation ceases. The planets take off energy from the sun equal to their gravital strength and give back to the sun through sun attractions as they receive. Waste of sun energy through radiation is simply a scientific fable. Radiating forces fade away in darkness while attracting forces come under currents on radial lines, giving light and heat from their interior work in bodies of matter resisting their flow.

Thus the action and reaction, the attraction and repulsion of the force currents environing matter are dominant over matter in all of its states and lines of motion. These forces of electricity and magnetism wrought into one great unified environment of the great world spheres uphold and move them as though held in the sensitive grasp of Omnipotence; insomuch that planetary velocities rival the flying radiance of the sunbeam and sensation is as delicate between sun and planets as between lovers at their bridal altar.

With matter in charge of these sovereign and universal forces there is nothing great nor nothing small. There is an infinite unity and infinitesimal diversity, giving an immeasurably grand personality of sensitive potency, divisible into distinct material personalities, each complete in itself and held in charge of its native environment, whether it be the mustard seed of the garden or the sun with its retinue of worlds.

With our old ideas of matter clouding our mental vision we find it a difficult task to peer into the shadowy realms of those material creative forces that close down around the initial centers of all forms of being and of life, with the inspiring touch of an inbreathing life force giving the sensitive imprint of paternity to every germ of organic development. We have been accustomed to think of living forms as created and put into their environment, and the thought of their natural birth from their environment is treated by the most of our great schools of learning with derision.

But the potter and the clay must come together to form the rudest vessels, so creative material forces must touch every sensitive atom that passes into organic being and keep the well-springs of life constantly flowing through all life forms. There is surely a material providence over all moving bodies, and all living forms of being, that is infinite in its outreaching measures, and finite in its everywhere visible forms of creative work, and in its watch-care of everything that has life and motion. There is no life without gravitation binding to place, and fixing germ centers. There is no unfolding of buds and blossoms, and rearing the tender shoots of vegetable, shrub or tree preparing the parental home of seed germs, and thus bearing fruit for the nourishing of animal life, without the going and coming of sunlight and earth-light, and the traveling of the earth in its annual journeys around the sun, and its diurnal revolutions giving day and night, cold and heat, causing winds and clouds, evaporation and condensation, by means of which the earth is watered with raindrops, and the fountains of the rivers are kept constantly flowing. All forms of life must have an environment of living forces, as truly as a constant supply of food for the sustaining of life. The beginnings of life are to be expected in all conditions where the continuance of life is possible, and hence the waters and the rivers, the planes and the mountains, throughout the different zones of the earth, up to the snow line of perpetual winter, reveal forms of life suited to all of their varied conditions of physical environment. The immanence of a sensory presence pervading all bodies of matter alike, whether world spheres or seed germs, with their inwrapt conditions of life, is as self-revealing in the world of matter as is the indwelling presence of life in the living bodily organism.

Life is, upon the elevated plane of the forces, where light, heat and moisture hold communion, a receptive center of atomic sensations that gives an organic continuance, as an initial beginning of a personified existence.

It is under the centralizing dual forces of a magnetic

field that atoms seek their affinities in the radiant glow of broken sun forces and earth forces,—thereby evolving light and heat, and a preparation for a place in organic structure.

Life forces and life forms touch each other as co-ordinates of being, under the sensitive touch of magnetic attractions and repulsions, that give to all life forms their environment of personal sensations, that constitute personality of being.

This environment of life that is purely an environment of occult material forces, must have its place around and permeating every living organism. It is the source of being and of strength, and also the cause and the courier of all the sensations of life. Failing to recognize this environing field of forces that give their attendance around everything having life, philosophers have failed to discover in matter the material basis of life.

We have already noticed the sovereignty of these forces over sun and planets, upholding and revolving them in space, and their commanding presence over all evolving forms of life, but we have only glanced at their working presence in the field of sensation, from which we acquire all true wisdom.

Without the sensory touch of material forces, there is no language with which Nature can reveal herself to mental vision. As evidence of this it may be noted that there are no symbols in any divine revelation expressed in religious creeds, that convey thought to the soul outside of the cognizance of the senses. Hence, some of the visions given us in books of popular imprint respecting a future life, tell us of what may be seen, heard, felt and enjoyed in a world of spirits, where mind is clothed in spirit form, as though spirit forms were enswathed in a material environment. Pure mental conceptions are all gained from the teachings of the senses. Material and mental forces meet together upon the plane of human consciousness. The language of the soul as told in visions, is the language of the here, applied to the hereafter.

Now it becomes a query among philosophers as to Nature's methods of communication between the material and the mental within the human brain.

The transference of sensation, as expressed in the so-called light of the sun, from sun to earth, unfolding to mental vision within the dark chambers of an animal brain, an accurate pictorial representation of every object touched by the light within the range of the eye; also the transference of sound from a disturbed center with accurate intonation, repeating in the ear-chambers of the brain of all animals within the disturbed area of sound, the exact expression at first uttered, though seconds may intervene between the uttering and receiving, or repeating, gives one of the most difficult problems of physical science. The wave theory of transmission of both light and sound, has taken too firm hold of the philosophy of the present age to be influenced by any criticisms from the pen of an unknown writer; and hence, I shall simply set over against this theory, the theory of central environments of force currents, as covering the whole field of creative and transmissive potencies.

And first, let it be noticed that light, heat and motion must be classified as properties of the forces, while atmosphere upon earth and sun, and ether of space must be classified as organic matter.

Again we have regarded light, heat, electricity, magnetism and gravity as different expressions of the dual working forces, in matter and pervading space, of attraction and repulsion—equal, and mutually reacting, giving the central linear radial lines of attraction, and the orbital right angled motion of repulsion. By thus reaching the work of the creative and governing forces of astronomical science in the linear currents of the electro-magnet we learn that central attraction, orbital repulsion, light, heat and motion belong to the environing forces of the magnet.

We also learn that the normal field of these forces, where they lay foundation structures and build around them central suns and revolving worlds, is at the low plane of the cold and darkness.

Central attractions and orbital repulsions grouped in a net-work of forces constitute a gravital, or magnetic field around each revolving sphere in the sun's system of worlds, and thus satellites and planets are revolved and floated in their orbits of motion, in the charge of these forces, so evenly and silently that astronomers discover neither retardation nor discord in the sun's system of worlds during the ages passed.

Thus, electro-magnetic environment is gathered around worlds from free space, from which also the solid spheres have themselves been formed under the charge of environing forces. In short, electro-magnetic atoms are built into electro-magnetic spheres out of electro-magnetic space and environed by electro-magnetic balancing currents of force that uphold and guide them in all of their orbits of motion. The where and the what of both matter and its commanding forces are self-conditioning elements of infinite space, only submitting to sensible measures in their mutual relations to aggregating centers of form and environment.

With these conceptions of matter and force and the materiality of space, sensation is mutual between organic bodies of matter and their environing forces. Sensations from space permeate bodies of matter and bodies of matter respond giving back sensations to space. Sunlight and earthlight, sun gravity and earth gravity are sensory impulses between sun and earth across the millions of miles of free space separating them, while the solid bodies of earth and sun take in such impulses and give back as they receive. No ether, star dust or cometary nebulous matter cuts any figure with such world forces, neither do any conflagrations rage among the waste baskets of these forces to make molten centers for new worlds, for they have no wastes, and Nature never builds out of the slag and crusts of matter floating on molten billows, consuming the spoiled work of chaos and darkness.

The pictorial etchings of the light are secured by linear vibrating currents passing from object to object, touching every object with responsive sensations that blend into an environment of sensations alike to every object within the illuminated field. The sensations of the entire field of vision thus pass into the eye and give their etchings upon the sensitive brain, giving accurate delineations of every object within the range of vision at a single touch and by a single impulse of the radiance of sensation which we call light.

The same radiant impulses of sensation that bring light to the eye also bring sound to the ear, and to every ear within the reach of sensations from a resonant center.

The patience of the reader may be sorely tried by the infelicities of language in which I have clothed my thoughts, but it should be noted that we are threading our way in new fields of mental vision, and the stumbling blocks of false theories are not only between the writer and his theme but between writer and reader.

I find but few aids in my lines of thought from the scientific vocabulary of the schools, and hence it becomes difficult to reveal the language of the occult forces in the philosophical language of those who teach that matter is dead and inert while all living forms of being are a divine creation.

In my efforts to extend the boundaries of human thought so as to visualize the foundations of the earth as they now appear in astronomical science, laid upon the sun's environing forces so firmly "that it should not be moved forever," I have endeavored to note the natural lines of the great archaic builder of suns and planetary worlds. These lines are plumb lines and right angled horizontal lines. The plumb lines of gravity with a right angled plane or level cutting them at any point that may be taken upon the earth's surface, give to the engineer lines that must be rigidly observed in all plants for the utilizing of mechanical power. The architect must build all his structures guided by the plumb line and level. The trees all grow upon plumb lines, while at their base the earth is relatively a plane but really a sphere. Rocks, seas and oceans are laid in their native beds at right angles to the plumb lines of environment.

These same radial and orbital lines of natural forces and power upon the earth, I have assumed, give the lines of the unseen forces that hold sun and planets in charge and give them their paths of motion. I do not intend to say that God did not build the world, but I do mean to say that when it was built it was built under the charge of gravital and orbital lines of material force currents. The work done proclaims the attraction and repulsion of these two companion forces of power as creators and governors of all worlds and all things having form and life.

In pursuing my line of thought the careful reader cannot fail to detect the points of divergence that I have made from the teachings of the old masters, and it is desired that these points of departure from old lines of philosophic reasoning should be well considered and their bearings taken upon advanced discoveries in the invisible realms of material creative forces.

Let it be noticed, therefore,

1. That we regard matter, as it appears in its sensible measures, in a secondary state which it has assumed under the sovereignty of material forces that are eternal and that have presided over all material changes of matter from atomic elements to revolving worlds.

2. That matter in its elementary state is as invisible and intangible as are the forces that determine all of its laws of motion and methods of work or aggregation.

3. Elementary matter and elementary space are measures of each other, and hence, all laws of motion are from matter in its atomic or invisible state and consequently are as universal as are gravity, matter and space.

4. Straight and curvelinear lines of motion are fixed by the innate impulse of all atoms of matter that gives sensible measures of attraction and repulsion. Attraction gives straight line radial motion toward centers of aggregation, while repulsion gives orbital lines of transference of both atomic elements and aggregations in body.

5. The order of creation is from motion to rest, from space to body, from velocities like the light to those of the planets in their orbits, and the most insignificant form of germ life.

6. The great spheres of matter that are gathered in sun systems of worlds are upheld and directed by the great sea of elementary forces from which they have been gathered.

7. The energy of attraction stored up in each planetary body is balanced by an environing field of orbital repellent forces that are an exact measure of its radial currents of attracting energy.

8. The conservation of energy arises from the conserved balance that the forces of attraction and repulsion mutually fix and preserve in all currents of moving forces.

9. The gravital centers of all planetary bodies and their orbital paths of motion are determined by these correlate and constantly acting sovereignties of matter in space.

10. Molecular forces find their methods of work accurately established under this balance of forces, insomuch

that perfect order and material harmony pervade the entire field of universal potencies and of elementary and organic forms of matter.

By molecular forces we do not mean forces constituted of loose floating forms of minute particles of matter, but of those forces that take on the linear form of the sunbeam and work through and around organic matter as the currents of force environing the magnet.

11. Light and heat are evolved from broken lines of electro-magnetic or gravital forces and are only revealed at such points in electro-magnetic currents of force as organic matter in some form interposes resistance to their normal flow in closed circuits of responsive floods of impulse.

a. The light and heat of creation are at such points and upon such planes of resistance as the dual floods of sun currents and earth currents are intercepted and broken by the resisting atmosphere of both earth and sun.

b. The rapidly revolving bodies of earth and sun by their gravital attractions take up these broken floods in their warm and glowing lines of energy and carry them to their place in all growing forms, and in all aggregating bodies of matter over which they cast their silvery mantle.

c. Attractions of earth and sun individualize and apportion the light and heat derived from these gravital-currents of energy according to the capacity of each body to absorb or take up their floods of elementary matter and energy.

d. Spectrum analysis reveals to science, in these lines of gravity in their glowing form, those substances that are built into earth, sun, stars and their families of worlds. Sunlight, earth-light and starlight tell the story of the bodies of matter and forms of life that they have built into place from their perennial sources of creative potencies, and the story of a single revolving world is the story of all worlds.

e. The light and heat of combustion or oxidation is simply a reversal of the energy of attraction by its co-ordinating energy of repulsion by which matter is broken up into currents and taken up into its native electro-magnetic floods in space.

CHAPTER VIII.

ACROSS THE BORDER.

WITH the coming of the Telephone and the Phonograph, we may look for a reconstruction of our methods of philosophical reasoning and scientific experiment.

The time has come when the errors of scientific deductions will be corrected by the illuminating presence of facts and forces that appear in the field of intellectual vision and at the same time elude all tests of material measure. The dividing line between spiritual and material forces and identities is now pushed farther back than mere sensible measures, so that where we once thought an infinite spirit wrought, we now detect the perfect order and working presence of material potencies.

The voice of the thunder is no longer to the world the voice of God, and the rainbow appears after the rain as a beautiful revelation of a material energy that commands all material changes in their order.

We are just beginning to learn that great material potencies of matter are veiled from the perceptions of the senses, and at the same time may become fully revealed to the sublime tests of human reason. Hence we have thought of spontaneous generation, of the evolution of all material substances and orders of being from one grand material energy. We find that human consciousness and human thought are cradled and nurtured in the embrace of physical forces, and that the law of primogeniture is commanded by a grand procession of material agencies that give tone and character to each line of progression. We are forced to the conviction, that if thinking orders of being were the offspring of spiritual conceptions, material energy caught up the conceptions and wrought out the perfected births, establishing with the species a line of marvelous forces that make it no sacrilege to class them with primary creative potencies.

The materialism of our scientific teachers and some of our schools of science will lose its objectionable features when new discoveries give to matter its marvelous sources of life and capabilities of creative wisdom. We call matter "dead, inert and insensate", because we have simply acquainted ourselves with the works of matter, ignoring the material agencies that have wrought with the elements of all life and form.

The delicate sensibilities, untiring patience, cunning artifice and sublime power of the working forces in matter, coupled with exact obedience to periods of time and mathematical order, can but inspire the thoughtful investigator with feelings akin to worship.

Elementary forces of matter and elementary forms, declare that "beginning" when creation's centers were fixed, and time began, and they compass the entire period, and determine all forms of creative work. We find the creative power and formative agencies of matter in the atomic elements. Both the builders and the materials for building, belong to matter, dissociate and inorganic, in space, and yet moving in systematic order and with the velocity of the light.

When we assign creative work to such a beginning, passing by nebulous matter and dead chaotic material as belonging to the age of dreams, then the most perplexing problems of creation will find an easy solution. Then a Tyndall will not endeavor to test the generative forces of matter with his animal and vegetable infusions, his pipettes and dark cabinets, from which are cut off the necessary conditions of life, and from such experiments, declaring in the face of the teeming millions that are generated, born, nurtured and sustained by material agencies, that "matter has in it no spontaneous generative power." Neither will a Crooks attempt to weigh the light, which will then appear as itself a balance of two grand correlate forces that hold all of matter in their joint embrace. Then the perplexing problems of world building, first causes, and sources of sun energy, will find a solution as simple as the circulation of fluids or the revolutions of the seasons.

In confirmation of these statements it is impossible to do more in these papers than to point to the opening door through which human thought must enter to reach the field of new discoveries. I have already intimated that we cannot pass present boundaries of scientific research in the use of the usual appliances of scientific experiment. The microscope and the telescope with their wonderful powers have led us hitherto, but the sweep of their power is limited.

They can afford us no assistance in fixing the periods

and discovering the measuring lines of the elements and energy that antedate material creations.

That self-confident pilot of unknown seas of thought, Joseph Cook, of the Boston platform, sweeps the heavens with his telescope and searches out organized bodies of matter in their minutest forms with his microscope, and then stops at the boundaries thus reached by the aid of his glasses, and affirms, "that beyond his horizon of observation there is a somewhat," and presuming he has reached the boundaries of material elements and forces, he teaches "that the somewhat must be the someone."

This is simply reaffirming the teachings of old mythologies, that the gods dwelt just outside of the firmament that limited human vision. It is only thus that our modern scientists become profane to the unlettered, while they bring to us no new revelations of the somewhat or the someone. Here we must pause unless we can extend discovery into the now hidden fields of elementary atoms, and primal material energy.

Modern research has attempted to reveal the methods of Nature in the formation of the great globes of matter, as well as in the organic structures of the mineral, vegetable and animal kingdoms of creation. The chemistry of science has furnished the educated mind with an acquaintance with the supposed elements of world-building.

Names are given to such elements and their varied endowments of energy and capacity are so definitely fixed in the family of material elements that their presence and work may be traced in the various organisms into which they enter. But chemical tests of the most delicate character by no means lead us to the boundaries of elementary forms and of elementary material energy. It is deserving of special notice, that as organisms are taken down and elements are reached, that power is developed.

The laboratory of the chemist is stocked with elements of unmeasured and unmeasurable energy. *e. g.* Water in its organic form is used as a mechanical power but its power is simply the power of a falling weight. It does work by its so-called inertia. Commence the work of dividing water, of dissociating its molecular forms by heat, producing steam, and then it does work by the repulsion of its atoms and thus becomes a source of power. Carry the process still further; gather its gases under the work of a galvanic battery and you have liberated three powerful working and building elements of matter, *viz.*, oxygen and hydrogen gas and electrical energy. Each of these elements possesses great working power and enters into organic structures as self-working agencies. These elements are only revealed in the laboratory of the chemist. They do their work in Nature as invisible forces, and yet without them organic matter could not be produced.

The chemist tells us that "all atoms of matter are regarded as originally charged with either positive or negative electricity." A molecule of water is made up of a positive atom of hydrogen, and a negative atom of oxygen. The quantity of electricity thus combined or neutralized in almost all kinds of matter is enormous. Faraday has stated that "a drop of water contains more than is discharged in the most violent flash of lightning."

From these statements let us fix definitely in mind,

1. That matter in its organic forms is held at rest under powerful atomic attractions. It is, in its solid state, the coiled spring, the suspended weight, of atomic power.

2. That when attraction gives way to repulsion and the elements of organization are released from body they pass to their home in space, marvels of energy.

3. That as matter becomes passive in organization and energetic in its elements, it follows that all of matter is organized and controlled by elementary forces, and that all of world building must be from atoms to combinations, from space to body.

4. That it is illogical and unscientific to pause at the boundaries of experiment with the forms of matter, and affirm that the "somewhat" that is hidden in the elements of matter is non-material, as the "someone."

Let it be borne in mind that we are desirous of guiding scientific thought to the opening door of logical demonstrations that acquaint us with material creative potencies that are native to the heretofore accredited home of spiritual agencies.

Not that we would discard the "someone," but that we would magnify the sublime power and infinite perfections of the "somewhat."

As chaos and nebulous matter reduced to globes of light in a grand primary conflagration have so long held place in the popular mind as the first stages in world formations, we must here pause to note the distinction between the work of elementary forces as builders and as destroyers, as organizing and disorganizing agencies. There is no question but the same forces that preside over attractions and aggregations of matter in body, also preside over repulsions and disorganizations of body.

Light and heat hold a commanding position among these agencies. Dr Draper, of New York, in his scientific memoirs says "A sickly looking plant springs from a seed in the dark. It is etiolated, as botanists say. If we examine it carefully, making allowance for the water it contains, we shall find that no matter how tall it may be, its weight has not increased beyond the original weight of the seed from which it came. It has been developing at the expense of the seed, the substance of which has been suffering exhaustion for its supply of nourishment. We cannot continue this development in the dark indefinitely, for the seed supply is soon exhausted and the shoot dies," p. 178. Again, we find on page 187 the following question and answer. "Whence has the force which manifests itself as heat and light in a flame been derived? Force cannot be created; it cannot spring forth spontaneously out of nothing. The answer is, it came from *the sun.*" Again he says on page 168, "The rays of the sun are the authors of all organization." Now we can but accept these emphatic declarations of this careful experimenter as final, as to the organic energy of the light and heat of the sun. But in our inquiries into the primary conditions of matter, we shall find it highly important that we note the radical distinction between light and heat as an organizing energy, and as a disorganizing energy; for the former must take precedence, in order of work, of the latter; and more than this, light and heat must as an organizing agency have a place in organic power before the sun himself became the chief reservoir of power in the sun-system. According to the line of thought we have been pursuing, elements and energy have woven their lines of organic power as truly into the body of the sun as into earth and planets; and they must have wrought systematically and in harmonic order from the beginning. Hence, before a universe of matter could be wrapped in a sea of flame, it must have been organized by a sea of forces. This leads to the thought, that the light and heat of the sun constitute a flame that never consumes; that they command a building energy and conserve that they have built.

The statement of Dr. Draper, "That the rays of the sun are authors of all organization," holds us firmly to the position that the flame of the sunbeam that always builds and never consumes, must have held a commanding place in organic world structures before the flames could be kindled that are fed from wasting organic forms.

And here we must express our regret that we are compelled to pursue a line of investigation that leads us into conflict with some of the popular scientific theories of the present time, among which is that of organic waste of the sun as source of light; and as failure to discover the true source of light will baffle all our efforts to solve the difficult problems of elements and elementary forces, we shall pursue our subject with only such reference to popular teachings as shall serve to make our positions clear to other minds. As it is conceded by all that light leads the forces in creative work, our attention must be fixed upon its source of power and its methods of work as our guides in the new fields of discovery into which modern thought is anxiously pressing.

Prof. Tyndall says ".The life of the experimental philosopher is two-fold. He lives, in his vocation, a life of the senses, using his hands, eyes, and ears in his experiments, but such a question as that now before us carries him beyond the margin of the senses. He cannot consider, much less answer the question "What is light?" without transporting himself to a world which underlies the sensible one, and out of which, in accordance with rigid law, all optical phenomena spring. To realize this subsensible world, if I may use the term, the mind must possess a certain pictorial power. It has to visualize the invisible. It must be able to form definite images of the things which that subsensible world contains, and to say that, if such a state of things exist in that world, then the phenomena which appear in ours, must, of necessity grow out of this state of things."

According to the above line of progressive thought we must attempt the solution of the problem of sunlight in harmony with the fact of sun-creation. To do this we must first gain a conception of light as an energy of a world of matter in an unorganic state, and as light now illuminates all matter in body, we conclude that its energy touched and guided all elements of matter in their atomic state. But we find that light is an organizer of matter in body, and we therefore may think of space as pervaded with the organic lines of light, holding in their sensitive embrace all elements of world-building.

With this conception of light in its elementary organic work, a logical sequence awakens the thought that from the beginning all of matter rests firmly in the embrace of the invisible energy of space, and that the order of creation must be from space to organic forms in body, and that the process must have been carried forward in perfect order. No chaos, no inertia, no insensate atom, no destruction, no waste, no loss by friction, no fortuitous gathering of dead atoms to be molded into form by plastic hands. It also follows that all bodies of matter, from primary molecular forms to the largest sun-spheres, are kept well in hand of the sovereign, invisible, material energy of space, and that all world velocities, and all orders of motion are under the guidance of such energy. The energy of atoms in space is the energy of atoms in aggregations of matter in body, and such energy works as freely in the hardened steel as in the softest sunbeam.

We refer to light as the invisible agency in creative work, because the visible radiance is but a single glowing point in the great circles of its power, and we desire to reach beyond the radiance of sun-energy in our estimates of its sovereignty over matter.

CHAPTER IX.

FOURTH STATE OF MATTER.

THE discussion thus far has led us to the contemplation of a state of matter that our teachers of science have heretofore failed to recognize.

We learn from our philosophers "that there are three states of matter, the solid, the liquid, and the gaseous." Light, heat, attraction of gravitation, electricity and magnetism have been left out of the classification.

Now, if I am not mistaken in my authorities and modes of reasoning, matter in its lowest indivisible form is found in the electric and magnetic currents, and also in light and heat, so that matter in its change of states passes from the atomic or electro-magnetic, to the solid, with gaseous and liquid states intervening. So I beg the privilege of affirming that matter is found in four states, solid, liquid, gaseous and electro-magnetic.

These different states depend upon that dual energy of the magnet, attraction and repulsion, working through atomic affinities under the modifying influence of light and heat.

I am constrained to regard light and heat as modified states of electricity and magnetism, arising from their working union to matter, and gravitation the balancing sovereignty of all material energy. This position that I have taken years ago is strengthened by the late discoveries of J. Norman Lockyer and Prof. Crooks, of England. These eminent experimenters in physical science have almost simultaneously reached advanced positions in the division of the "elements," as they have been styled.

Mr. Lockyer has given the most careful study to spectra of the light-bearing globes, and he states, "That five years ago he pointed out that there are many facts and many trains of thought suggested by solar and stellar physics, which point to another hypothesis, namely, that the elements, or at all events some of them, are compound bodies."

Prof. Crooks from a different line of experiment reached a similar conclusion, and he announces a "fourth state of matter," which he styles the "ultra-gaseous."

It is with matter, then, in its fourth state that we are to seek an acquaintance as the somewhat that works outside of the boundaries of sensible measure.

And here we may pause and take a hasty sketch of the outlying fields of thought as they now appear. They are bounded by the somewhere of space and they are the somewhat that pervades the somewhere with infinite lines of energy moving with the velocity of the light and in harmonic order.

The conception we have gained of the fourth state of matter is that of an independent, self-necessitated and causative state. We cannot ask after source, boundaries or foundations of either the elements or the energy that sweep through space with the invisible flow of the electric and magnetic waves of counterflowing impulses.

The elements of matter in their infinitesimal forms and tenuity of structure reach the outermost boundaries of thought. Like space and gravity there is nothing thinkable beyond, beneath, above or before them.

From such a state may come all of the aggregations of matter and all of the forces that carry forward the transformations in its three other states. Attraction, like the power of falling weights, pulls the atomic forms of matter, like raindrops, towards the gravital centers of the great globes of space, and repulsion lifts again the mists of the great oceans and the wastes from the decaying forms of matter back again to a place among the elements from which they have been taken. It is to be noted that light, heat, electricity and magnetic energy are the transmuting and carrying forces of matter in all of its changes, and I may also add in all of its grand velocities and paths of revolution around gravital centers.

CHAPTER X.

UNITY OF THE FORCES.

IN Prof. Tyndall's work on "Heat" considered as a "Mode of Motion", page 225, he says "We have every reason to conclude that heat and electricity are both modes of motion; we know experimentally that from electricity we can get heat, and from heat, as in the case of our thermo-electric pile, we can get electricity. But although we have, or think we have, tolerably clear ideas of the character of the motion of heat, our ideas are very unclear as to the precise nature of the change which this motion must undergo in order to appear as electricity—in fact, we know as yet nothing about it."

Thus, then, we are to look to an acquaintance with light and heat as our only sure guides passing between the dark land of electric and magnetic velocities, to the land of light and sensible organic structures, and of still more wonderful velocities.

The experiments of our scientific teachers, as we have noted, lead us to the borders of the dark land of universal energy and universal motion—to the cold, deep darkness of stellar space pervaded with working lines of gravital energy and the so-called radial lines of light and heat energy, that move out from sun and stars to build in creation's great work-shops.

From this dark cold land, both the scientist and theologian must admit, have been gathered the great suns and sun-systems that now stud the heavens with their brilliant lights—ever burning and never consuming the bodies from which they shine. Out of such depths these great lights have been kindled and kept constantly burning. Within these depths have been fixed the great equatorial planes of the solar systems in which rest firmly the gravital centers of suns and planets, fixing the great north and the great south by the same lines that fix the points of the mariner's compass. Here then we are brought face to face with the great law of polarization of currents, working in space, back of the law of gravity. Polarization is the result of two compound forces. The two forces are electricity and magnetism, each compounded of the oppositely moving forces of attraction and repulsion, positive and negative currents. The forces of electricity and magnetism reveal themselves in the magnet, and we believe in all growing organisms of matter as equally balancing forces, always moving at right angles to each other and by so doing establishing axial lines and orbital lines of globes of energy of varied size, according to the strength of the nucleus centers that command them.

A completed circuit of either electrical or magnetic lines is constituted of double lines of energy—positive and negative—and according to the law of currents flowing freely in space, which is,—"That currents moving in the same direction attract, while those moving in opposite directions repel"—we must regard a completed circuit as made up of two oppositely revolving rings, each complete in its circuit of revolution, and yet bound to the other, each to each, by a magnetic lateral flow of impulses. This interflowing of electrical opposites in lines of energy in free space, is taught by experiment of currents with currents, and also is a necessity to the balance of positive and negative energy, in the gravital attractions that pass over the same space between planetary bodies. The radius-vector, a line joining the center of the earth with the center of the sun, and that in the revolution of the earth around the sun, describes the plane of equatorial rest, or equatorial calms, where both the centers of the planets rest, and the polar currents lose their strength, is the central line of two cones of forces that do constant work between the sun and earth, holding the earth to her orbit and also carrying from earth to sun and sun to earth by the same lines of attraction all the light and heat energy that passes between them. Between the two bodies must be an equal exchange of energy. The earth gathering by attraction from the sun through her cone of forces with a base of 852,000 miles in diameter, and its apex at the center of the earth, just as much strength as the sun gathers by his cone of forces 8,000 miles in diameter terminating at the sun's center. As these radial lines of attraction grouped in oppositely pointing altitudes of conical build, evidently constitute independent oppositely flowing attractions, there must have moved out from each body repellent energy, gathered into the same conical forms; otherwise sun and planet would be drawn together by mutual attractions. Such repellent energy is revealed in the electric orbital flood of currents that are grouped around the earth and that drive it along its path around the sun always at right angles to the radius-vector and also to all floods of energy passing between earth and along radial lines of attraction.

According to the vision we have gained of these forces, each solar system constitutes a vast globe of unified force-currents with two hemispheres—a north and a south, divided by an equatorial plane of permanent rest and perpetual calms.

In this vast globe of forces, the center of the sun is the revolving center with his solid nucleus of 850,000 miles in diameter, with a radiant envelope of light, and from these orbital and radial floods of energy extending to Neptune, the outermost planet in his family of worlds, enveloped in their hemispheres of forces the planets take their places, each with their hemispheres of matter and currents, with equatorial planes of rest coinciding with the equatorial plane of rest of the sun's forces. Add to this vision the thought that these hemispheres reveal their working strength in great polar attractions and repulsions, that are balanced so perfectly as to give to the vast equatorial plane of the sun's equator the stability of perpetual rest, and then there may be gained some conception of the exhaustless source of that mechanical power that upholds and keeps in perpetual motion in this great plane, that system of satellites and planets that revolve so harmoniously and in such perfect order of time around the sun.

The thoughts we have already fixed in mind respecting the power of the linear forces of this sun-sphere should be strengthened by a glance at their wonderful velocities. To do this refer to the swing of the pendulum of a clock beating seconds, and note that at each vibration the currents between the earth and sun move 182,000 miles and Mercury goes forward in his orbit 30.40 miles; Venus 22.24 miles; Earth 18.91 miles; Mars 15.32 miles, and Neptune at the distance of 2,272,325,000 miles from the sun, moves 3½ miles.

By noticing the decreased velocity of the planets in their orbits as they recede from the sun, it will be clear to any mind that neither primary divine impulse nor inertia will account for their uniform retardation.

From the views we have now gained of the working power of the polar and equatorial currents of the solar system we deduce these statements :

1. That the polar forces of the sun and planets establish the equatorial plane of rest in which the centers of gravity of the various bodies are evenly held. These forces in the magnet are called magnetic currents.

2. That the currents that pass around the earth, parallel to the equator, are repellent forces that drive the earth and planets across the radial lines of attraction that draw towards gravital centers of sun and planets, and by so doing determining the curvilinear paths of the planets. These currents in the electro-magnet are called electrical currents.

As we have before stated each class of currents is constituted of two oppositely moving polarizing currents of equal strength, called positive and negative.

Our position is that all matter is, in its fourth state held in these four divisions of the grand polarizing material energy of the entire universe consisting of its 64 elements.

In these polarizing forces matter is revealed in lines of infinitesimal fineness, and in two equally balanced divisions of virgin elements. The positive elements all flowing in positive currents and the negative all flowing in the negative currents. These floods always moving in opposite directions and in space are mutually repellent, never meeting though interflowing, of equal strength and equal velocities. We suggest the thought that the male and female distinction in generative organic forces here finds its primary cause. The classes of atoms that repel in space seek each other and join in firm embrace in all organic unions. Positive currents represent the male principle of mattei and negative currents the female principle.

Now we are to keep in mind that we are visualizing a system of harmoniously working forces, that are real working agencies in world formation; that they hold all forms of matter in their embrace and guidance, and yet make no report to the senses. They are the "co-ordinating forces that work back of the bioplasm arranging the growth of the whole body."

As Mr. Cook has well said, "If their influence were here in the air you could not touch it; you could pass your hand through it; you could not feel it, and yet you know it is there. But these nerves themselves were woven by the bioplasts. Take out the bioplasts. Let them retain their co-ordination. There is something behind them— the co-ordinating power. You know such a power is there. Take that co ordinating power out; hold it up here; you cannot see it, you cannot touch it, but it is there."

Again he says, "It is an accepted conclusion with Julius Muller that this finest thing of all, or the co-ordinating force which we know exists in the physical organism, is the true body." This unseen co-ordinating power as we have seen must weave its net-work of forces through every organic form. It presides over every generative embrace of either atoms or organic bodies of atoms. It traces out generative lines of order, preserves distinctions between all classes, individualizes form and being, gives continuity to life, and is the working power in all things that have life. Even the rocks in their crystalline structures and the metals in their solid forms are bound together by, and command the constant watchfulness of these unseen forces. Let not the reader be in haste to pass from these visions of creative power and of omnipotent strength that we have been contemplating as belonging to the material elements of creation. It is to these thoughts that we must recur again and again, to guide us in our discoveries of the wonder-working powers of matter in its invisible organisms.

[NOTE.] The reader will here notice that the writer's conception of the working unity of the forces was not clear at the writing upon the transference of energy, as light and gravity between sun and planets. There can be no radial lines of attraction separate from orbital lines of repulsion, and hence the chapters on gravity and planetary motion were subsequently written, to which the reader is referred for a more perfect delineation of the unity of the forces than is found in this chapter.

CHAPTER XI.

NATURE'S METHODS IN CREATION.

I NOW invite the attention of the reader who has kept company with me thus far to attempt to follow in vision the natural order that these invisible forces preserve in building up organic structures.

And the first step in the order is resistance awakened between energy and atoms.

The separating line between matter in its fourth, or electro-magnetic state and matter in its solid state, is the line of work fixed by resisting atomic attractions. These attractions spring from the lagging behind of overburdened electrical currents, in which magnetic, or cross currents, gain the mastery and establish gravital centers. When once established, resistance awakens magnetic strength, and magnetic strength increases atomic accretions and the work of building is established as a perpetual work. Matter in its organic form is bound together by the lateral attraction of atoms, while in free space they are joined by polar attractions; hence, the strength of a body of matter as it increases in magnitude is increased in the length and strength of its lateral and polar currents of attraction that draw matter on radial lines towards its gravital center. At the same point the electrical currents of space take up their work around the body of equal strength to the magnetic currents, and thus, matter in its various states, with its circle of transformations and changes, goes constantly forward.

We have already glanced at the gravital plane of rest that is established by the equatorial planes of each family of planets under the commanding influence of the great central sun.

In this great plane of rest the gravital center of each body of the solar system is held by equally balanced orbital forces, while at right angles to this plane of rest—common to the whole system of orbital forces and revolutionary motion—the poles of each revolving globe become fixed by a system of polar forces, so that each forming globe takes its place in space under the firm guidance of two grand forces that fix a grand plane of revolution and at right angles to such plane polar forces that establish axial centers of revolution.

This somewhat involved statement is here made that we may gain a comprehensive view of the systematic working energy, with which all of matter is brought into form and place in the progressive steps of world-building.

In this conception of the co-working of matter and energy in world creation it appears that there is an exact balance preserved between each body of matter and the working forces that have fashioned it. The sun's energy is felt by Neptune, the most distant planet in the solar system, at a distance of 2,770,247,000 miles. This energy moves in great circles around the sun, equal in strength to the magnitude of the attractions of matter built into the sun's body, and Neptune, whose light is vailed from our unaided vision, responds feebly to the sun's influence, and takes up its orbital march around the sun, traveling in its orbit with only one-sixth of the velocity the earth attains in her orbit.

Within the sun's great globe of unified and balanced currents, all the planets with their satellites, each surrounded by a like globe of forces clinging to their gravital centers, perform their wonderful revolutions and acquire their individual velocities. In scripture phrase it may be truly said, "In Him" they "live, move and have their being."

From the ideas we have here gained of the elements and forces that enter into the great work of world-creation, we are enabled to fix certain elementary principles of mechanical power by which the machinery of the solar-system is unerringly governed. And

1. The power rests primarily in two grand divisions of world energy, *viz.*, attraction and repulsion.

2. These two equal divisions of power are bound together by a neutral plan of rest as truly in the atom as in the great globes of matter; hence we have the polarized atom of the sunbeam as truly as the polarized bodies of sun, earth and planets.

3. The two forces of the solar system, attraction and repulsion, obey the great laws of polarization, and perform their work across and around the fixed planes and axial lines of motion; hence the equatorial plane of the sun's revolution becomes the equatorial plane of revolution of all the planets and polar forces fix axial centers of revolution at right angles to such plane of rest.

4. Centers of aggregation and of revolution are fixed

at the point of intersection of the poles of each planet with the great equatorial plane of the solar system.

[NOTE.] In the preparation of this chapter the writer had in mind the idea of orbital impulse as resulting from impact or projection of a right angled force as is given in the parallelogram of forces; but in the electro-magnetic balance, the right angled force resisting gravity is a right angled force of attraction. The earth revolves towards the line of flow of the electric currents around the earth; as matter is attracted toward the earth's center in radial lines, so the earth revolves toward the flow of attracting currents on the surface of the earth, and the planets in their orbits move towards the flow of the great orbital currents in environing space. Attractions toward the central body and attractions around a central body give a closed orbit of motion. Both forces are under the central energy of the body, through which and around which they attract. Hence it is, that all orbital lines are circles, and all orbits closed orbits, as these forces are jointly balancing forces of attraction, respecting at all times the same central bindings of their mutual strength. The repulsion of these joint forces is a pressure on all gravital lines from a center outward, as in the growth of an apple or in expansion of matter under pressure, as in the ignition of dynamite, also as appears in waves moving out from a disturbed center. In the attraction and repulsion of matter by the forces they act as a unit of force.

Thus we find the sun, with its family of planets, constituting a perfect system of machinery, self evolved, self-adjusted and self-moved, perpetually working out and revealing the manifold wonders of creation.

The machinery of the heavens has its beginning in the eternity past of atoms and energy, and has the promise of an eternity to come in its living wheels and immortal energy that co-exist and co-work without a lawless atom to disturb their harmony.

CHAPTER XII.

ATTRACTION AND REPULSION EQUAL FACTORS IN GRAVITATION.

WE now come to the study of the law of intercommunion between sun and planets.

We have been taught that the law of universal gravitation governs the motion of the planets in their orbits, and gravity, according to our text books, simply means attraction. The law is thus stated: "The force with which two material particles respectively attract each other is directly proportioned to their masses, and inversely proportioned to the square of the distances between their centers."

Here it will be seen that we have given us the law of descending weights, but no law of lifting weights. The law according to which the planets and all matter falls toward the sun, but no law of orbital energy by which planets are kept out of the sun, and these two forces must be balanced forces to impart the curvilinear motion that the planets take in their orbits around the sun.

In this diagram there is a representation of two equal forces working at right angles to each other thereby giving a curvilinear motion to the body acted upon similar to that of a planet in its orbit.

In this figure the body, acted upon by the single force of attraction would in a given time fall from and along the radial line *m c* to *a*, but it has described a curvilinear path, and reached *n* in the circle *m n*, hence a force equal to the attraction *m c*, must have been exerted upon the body

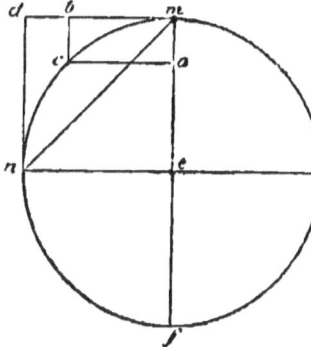

in the line *m b*, thus at every point in the circle *m n*, the two forces remain constant. From whence comes this repellent force balancing sun attraction? We have said that it comes from the repellent energy of atoms in space moving with the velocity of the light around all bodies of matter and at right angles to the radial lines of such bodies. The rule we here state thus, *atoms in body attract along radial lines towards gravital centers, atoms in space repel or resist attraction and take up their line of motion at right angles to the radial lines of attracting masses.*

Now as we have seen that repellent orbital energy surrounding a magnetic body is a balance to the attracting, axial or magnetic energy within it; the law of the atom governs the law of the forces that have it in charge; the same is the law of the great globes of matter.

But our teachers in philosophy have treated of matter as if it were dead, inert and plastic, and of the work of creation as if consisted in moulding such matter into bodily forms, and imparting life to such forms by a spiritual inbreathing; hence they teach that the orbital force of matter consists of an original, divine impulse given to matter at its creation which the inertia of matter still retains.

That neither original, divine impulse nor inertia has anything to do with the orbital force of planetary bodies is evident from the fact that the force of attraction of matter for matter reveals in it a universal energy, and denies the existence of such a law in matter as inertia, while it is irrational to suppose that original impulse should be imparted to matter as a balancing energy against a constantly pulling power of attraction.

Again the repellent energy of atoms is revealed in all chemical and mechanical unions as equal to attractions, so that matter is changed from solid to liquid, from liquid to gaseous, and from gaseous to electro-magnetic, solely by the use of material agencies. The weight that falls to the earth by attraction may be lifted by repulsion.

Matter by attraction comes to rest in body, by repulsion it springs, like an arrow from a bent bow, to its home in space. Again the process of growth in all living organisms is carried forward by the working energy of the two equal forces of attraction and repulsion. I hesitate not to affirm that all growing bodies are growing magnets, and that they are fed solely from atomic elements, that, gathered from sun-currents and earth-currents, move to their place in body under the guidance of magnetic attractions and repulsions. This is the life energy that works back of the pioplasms as we have already noticed.

And now we are brought face to face with the hitherto perplexing problem of waste and supply of sun energy. It is the great problem of astronomical science and hitherto has found no solution consistent with the perpetuity of the solar system. I state the problem as I find it in "Elements of Astronomy," by J. Norman Lockyer, a work now in use in schools, published in 1873. After referring to the sun as the source of light he says, "Then as to the sun's heat. The heat thrown out from every square yard of the sun's surface is greater than that which would be produced by burning six tons of coal on it each hour. Now, we may take its surface roughly at 2,284,000,000,000 square miles and there are 3,097,000 square yards in each square mile. How many tons of coal must be burnt, therefore, in an hour to represent the sun's heat?

"But the sun sends out, or radiates, its light and heat in all directions, it is clear, therefore, that as our earth is so small compared with the sun and is so far away from it the light and heat the earth can intercept is but a very small portion of the whole amount, in fact, we only grasp the $\frac{1}{2300000000}$ part of it. All the planets together receive but two hundred and twenty-seven millionths of the solar light and heat.

"The whole heat of the sun collected on a mass of ice as large as the earth would be sufficient to melt it in two minutes, to boil the water thus produced in two minutes more, and to turn it all into steam in a quarter of an hour from the time it was first applied.

"Will the sun keep up forever a supply of the force that has been described? It cannot, if it be not replenished, any more than a fire can be kept up unless we put on fuel; any more than a man can work without food. At present philosophers know not by what means it is replenished. As, probably, there was a time when the sun existed as matter diffused through space, the condensation of which matter has stored up its heat, so probably, there will come a time when the sun, with all its planets welded into its mass, will roll a cold black ball, through infinite space;" and then follows this remarkable statement:

"We have no evidence, however, of any loss of heat, even from century to century, and if there is a loss there will doubtless be sufficient heat left to supply the planets with all they need for thousands of years to come."

Now, by turning to the estimate of the sun's mass compared with all the planets and we find that the sum in miles of the diameters of all the planets multiplied by three is 100,000 miles less than the diameter of the sun. This, surely, does not comport with the theory that the sun's wasting energies have for ages been supplying building material for the bodies of the planets.

Again Mercury receives seven times more light and heat from the sun than the earth, and yet its diameter is nearly two-thirds less than that of the earth, while Jupiter receives many times less light and heat than the earth and has a diameter more than ten times greater, and a volume 1,400 times greater. These comparisons teach us that the great law of waste and supply of sun energy in dispensing light and heat to the planets is not such as is presented in the problem that our astronomers have found so difficult of solution.

To correct the statement in accordance with the hypothesis and arguments of this paper, I state,

1. That the light and heat of both sun and planets are building forces on the surfaces of their several bodies.

They illuminate and warm the bodies to which they cling but never consume them.

2. Each planet in the solar system holds its place in its orbit under the great law of gravital attractions and according to this law the sun attracts matter to its own body on radial lines and never radiates either light or heat as a supply to planetary bodies. According to the same law every revolving body in the solar system attracts matter to itself according to its mass or volume, and its light and heat will be in proportion to its strength of magnetic attractions. Neither sun nor moon are exceptions to this law.

Waiving the discussion of the question of light and heat other than that of incandescence, which will in its place aid materially in our conclusions, let us pass to notice the testimony of the light as to its lines of propagation from body to body. And

1. The light moves in straight lines, whether radiated, attracted or reflected.

2. In passing from a solid lump of coal to its electromagnetic state by means of combustion or repulsion, it radiates from the center of propagation to the vanishing lines of its sphere of illumination.

3. In building itself into the solid mass of coal it obeyed the law of attraction and moved in straight lines towards the gravital center of the growing organism that attracted it.

From these statements we notice that the lines of light coincide with the lines of gravital attractions and consequently in creation move on radial lines towards gravital centers, and in combustion take up the same lines of motion in reversed order.

Also, that in reflection it obeys the law of an elastic falling body, preserving still its perfect linear order of motion.

Now let us select from the great circles and the great globes of the solar system, the straight lines of any mathematical figure we may construct, whether circles, spheres, cones or sections of cones and they will be radial lines and none other. We have here then, the elucidation of the principle of evolution of light and heat from the gravital attraction of falling bodies, when encountering a resisting medium. We have stated that the radial lines of light and heat as they come to us from space, or as we say, from the sun, follow gravital lines of attraction. If this be so, they obey the law of falling bodies, and yet upon the surface of the earth, evolve light and heat, which upon the earth are repellent forces.

But note again that we have regarded these radial lines as magnetic lines, laden with the virgin elements of matter, and that illumination of these elements is awakened by the resistance of the atmosphere on the surface of body upon which they fall. Again, the breaking up and disturbance of these radial lines of attraction, awaken also electrical lines of repulsion, and in the vibrating swing of the commingling currents of electrical and magnetic lines of energy, light and heat are evolved. Earth and sun giving the electro-magnetic couple that completes the circuit of electric conduction.

Then we have reached the grand ideal of our scientist,

by a wholly different line of thought, involving different scientific conclusions, *viz.*, "That the light and heat of the sun are supplied from gravital energy pouring virgin atoms of matter into the sun's atmosphere," thus evolving his brilliant light and heat within his own photosphere.

But in all of this there is no waste of energy, no force of incandescence to light other globes, no radiation of heat into cold, dark, unrequiting space, no evidence of decaying suns or burned-out worlds. Every planet by this law of evolution shines with its own light, measured by its gravital energy, and warms itself from the source that supplies its ever growing strength, and unfolding orders of creative work.

The power that appears upon the earth as sunlight is thus awakened within the earth's atmosphere and like the power of gravity gives back to the sun just as much as it receives.

CHAPTER XIII.

SOURCES OF LIGHT AND HEAT.

IN review of the theory we have discussed in this paper, "making the lines of light and heat identical with gravital lines of attraction," it will be noticed that the enlightening energy of the earth upon the sun is conveyed in lines gathered in the form of a cone, consequently upon the sun's equator circles of light are presumed to fall corresponding to the magnetic or gravital energy of the various planets. These circles of illumination will follow upon the equator of the sun, the motion of the planets as the moon's shadow falls upon the earth at an eclipse of the sun. Confirming this theory I quote a short article upon the "variability of the sun's surface," from the "Supplement Scientific American, No. 161." "At one of the sessions of the French Association, Jenssen described the apparatus which enabled him to take photographs with an exposure of $\frac{1}{100000}$ of a second, and explained the new information which such photographs have furnished respecting the upper surface of the photosphere. The polar regions are covered with a general granulation of forms, dimensions and distributions very different from the ideas which have been derived from optical examination. Resemblances to willow leaves, rice grains, etc., may be occasionally traced in single points, but the prevailing and fundamental form is spherical, and the 'grains' appear to be clouds of dust or mist floating in a gaseous medium. The luminous intensity of the sun resides chiefly in a few points, so that if the whole surface was as bright as the most brilliant portions, its luminosity would be increased from ten to twenty fold."

This photographic appearance of the sun is wholly inconsistent with the teaching that the sun is a burning mass and a radiator of light and heat for the use of the planetary bodies of the solar system, and to say the least, is not inconsistent with the theory of electro-magnetic illumination of the heavenly bodies, as has been presented in this paper.

The deferred subject of light and heat, of vital interest in this discussion, now demands attention and must be compressed into as narrow limits as possible; outlines of our argument only, can be given. And

1. The reader must be reminded that our subject brings us again to the border land of the senses, where we must seek an acquaintance with the unseen and intangible by actualizing in our mind images of thought. Our books of science teach us that the "sun is the source of light and heat and of all power." We answer, no, and say that light and heat energy must have existed before the first atoms of sun-formation were bound together. The sun surely is large enough to be the sensible source of light and heat, but what of the invisible energy that has stored itself up in the sun's vast organism? By experiment we find light is motion. It moves with inconceivable velocity. It traverses space and comes to the eye in lines of

infinite fineness, and envelopes all things that have life in its silvered mantle. It brings with it warmth and building energy, also the atoms of matter of which sun and planets are built. We are taught by analysis of the sun's light, that in its fine drawn lines are sodium, iron, magnesium, barium, copper, zinc, calcium, chromium, nickel, and if these, why not all elements of matter? Again, while it comes to us laden with matter, it has no perceptible weight, and therefore must be a balanced energy such as gravity is, that carries great globes of matter in equally poised balances, woven of two great hemispheres of forces.

Again, it shines from out of the cold, deep darkness of stellar space, and grows strong by resistance and only puts on its shining garments of visible form when it has work to do, either in lifting up the tender shoot just emerging from its seed in the earth, or in riving and crushing the sturdy tree of the plain.

It carries with it all power over life and form in matter and yet nurtures into life the tiniest seed that falls upon the earth, and more, it wraps up all forms of coming life in the buds, blossoms and seeds of the present.

We learn also that the invisible rays that accompany the light rays, have more heating and chemical energy than the visible, so we conclude that the true source of light and heat is invisible, intangible, and as exhaustless as space is unlimited. It is under the working power of that energy that appears as light and heat, that matter is carried through all of its changes of state, and takes on all of its forms of power.

We have already seen, that according to the everywhere

working lines of polarization, that both matter and energy are equally divided into two hemispheres of form, and bound together at a neutral equator of rest. We have also found the positive and negative currents of space moving side by side in opposite directions, mutually repellent, virgin elements.

Now the central thought that must guide us in dealing with light and heat, is, that they are primarily revealed at the change of matter from its electro-magnetic state in space to its magneto-electric state in body.

At the joining where currents are broken up into atoms, and where positive and negative atoms take up a generative union, or at least freely commingle on the surface of body, there light and heat are developed, conversely when friction is applied to matter in mass, or concussion disturbs violently its atomic structure, thereby disturbing the equilibrium of the dual correlate forces of attraction and repulsion that are a constant presence in all organized bodies of matter, repulsive energy is awakened and heat is evolved. The work of repulsion is manifest in the expansion of the disturbed body, and if the disturbed mass is subjected to a sufficiently persistent friction or concussion, light succeeds heat, repulsion overcomes attraction, and combustion marks the vanishing line across which the divided atoms pass to their linear structure in space.

Thus when matter comes to rest under the prevailing energy of attraction, it passes from the cold, dark condition of currents through a resisting medium, to the electro-magnetic balance of light, and, on the contrary, when disorganization takes place, it passes again through a like electro-magnetic balance of atoms to a new organization in body or to its home in space.

The power under which these changes in matter are carried forward is its power of attraction and repulsion of matter in its linear condition.

The summit-level upon which these opposing forces relinquish their mutual burdens in creative work is that of the light. Through its shining portals all of matter passes, whether seeking rest in body or ceaseless activity in space. In the electric light the power that is revealed in the flame is at the dark ends of the carbon pencils, and has its source in the positive and negative impulses of either magnet or battery. We must then note clearly the distinction that experiment makes between light and heat and the dual power that feeds it from the invisible polarized floods of space, as we distinguish between the candle and the flame that derives its brilliancy from its wasting form.

When this distinction is clearly in mind, we shall then learn how to think of that dual organism of currents that is behind all organisms of matter, an invisible and still a guiding and sustaining power. Let the electro-magnet be our teacher and reveal to us the great mystery of its strength and we shall learn that an unseen material energy waits upon every living thing and gives strength to every organic form possessing power.

It is after this "something" that is back of sensible organic forms of matter that we are now searching. We take the electro-magnet in our hands, examine it, weigh it, and note its construction and test its power. It is a piece of round, soft iron, bent in the form of the letter u. The two ends of the iron we call poles, with reference to future use; the polar ends are wound with a copper wire wound with silk or thread so as to keep it separate by insulation from any connection with the iron. The opposite ends of the wire project beyond the poles of the magnet.

Thus far we are dealing with sensible measures. The weight of the iron, the length of the wire, etc., we fully understand, and yet there is an energy binding together the atoms of the metals from which the magnet has been constructed that eludes all sensible tests. These metals came into their present condition from the heated furnace a liquid, glowing with a repellent energy equal to the cohesive strength now binding together their atomic structure. Now what we are inquiring after is the balancing center of that conservation of energy in matter that does interior work and thus indicates its presence in all material attractions and repulsions that give form to body and work all transformations of matter. In prosecuting our inquiry we have set acids at work in our galvanic battery upon zinc and copper, taking down their organic structure atom by atom, and liberating the energy binding atoms in their metallic form. This energy we lead off by conducting wires that we join to the wires projecting from the poles of our prepared magnet, and when the current is completed electric currents flow through the wire around the soft iron bar, and at once an induced flow of magnetic currents pass through the magnet, pouring into each pole with equal velocity and strength of energy to the electric currents passing around the iron magnet in the conducting wire.

Apply to this magnet a soft iron keeper, joining the poles and completing the magnetic currents and our magnet lifts pounds. This power of the electro-magnet is the power of electro-magnetic currents, and is the same power of currents that do interior work in the metals binding them together by attraction, or taking them back to elementary atoms by repulsion.

In an extract from a memoir of Sir Humphrey Davy, on page 110 of Tyndall's work on "Heat as a Mode of Motion," we find this important statement; "The effects of the attraction of cohesion, the great approximating cause, on the corpuscles of bodies is exactly similar to that of the attraction of gravitation on the great masses of matter compassing the universe, and the repulsive force is analagous to the planetary projectile forces. He also says, "The particles of bodies may be considered as acted upon by two opposing forces; the approximating power, which may (for greater ease of expression) be called attraction, and the repulsive motion. The first of these is the compound effect of the attraction of cohesion by which the particles tend to come in contact with each other. The second is the effect of a motory or vibratory impulse given to them tending to remove them farther from each other, and which can be generated, or rather increased, by friction or percussion."

Thus it appears that in the mind of Sir Humphrey Davy there was a blending of the two compound forces of cohesive attraction, and projectile or heat repulsion, and the gravital planetary force of attraction and the projectile force of repulsion.

I desire to emphasize the thought that these forces are thus blended in Nature, and at the same time to note the conditions upon which they appear as light and heat, in contrast with the conditions in which they appear as simple planetary motion. And first we observe in the electromagnet that the two compound forces are divided by a never changing law into radial and orbital currents of energy. By increasing the strength of either the orbital or the axial currents the correlate currents will be equally increased, so that magnets have been constructed able to sustain many times their own weight, and yet while the currents are left to an unresisted freedom they balance each other and neither light or heat are evolved. In planetary motion this free balance is preserved and constant velocities and completeness of systematic revolutionary motion is preserved.

The repelling or projectile electrical currents and the attracting magnetic currents, establish a common gravital center and a common equator of rest, which, extended into space from such center at right angles to the axial currents, becomes the balancing plane of revolution.

But currents in free, unobstructed motion are still under perfect obedience to the law of current-polarization, which is, "that currents flowing in the same direction attract, while those moving in opposite directions repel," consequently positive and negative pass each other in their circuit of motion, each flowing at the rate of 180,000 miles in each second of time, making a compound motion of 360,000 miles per second. These counter flowing currents hold in their embrace all of matter in free space and constitute vast globes of systematized material energy. They also hold a gravital relation to matter in organic forms, bearing the great globes of space with an evenly balanced motion along their circular paths of perpetual journeyings. This state of matter in the field of its sublimest displays of creative wisdom and omnipotent power, is superior to sensible measure; its atomic forms and its floods of power are cold, dark, attenuate, and elude both touch and vision.

Now let the connection be broken between battery and magnet; its wonderful power is gone and it becomes as at first, simply iron and insulated wire. In the place of the magnet let a thin platinum wire be inserted, restore battery connections and we soon discover that the currents of the battery are working under new conditions. The platinum wire is a strong resistant in the pathway of the currents; their compound motion of 360,000 miles per second is arrested, and their oppositely moving currents, like oppositely moving trains of cars simultaneously meeting a grand obstruction, are broken up and piled together, and from the gravital concussion of atoms, thus dashing against the obstructing platinum wire, light and heat are evolved. The velocity of the dark currents of the connecting wires is now revealed in light and heat. In this new condition of energy new relations of matter succeed. Through the flame the atoms of the oppositely flowing currents are dashed into a new embrace; positive and negative seek each other in firm chemical unions, and by the attractions of aggregat matter are carried to their place in material forms. Through this order of resistance, concussion and generated repulsions and attractions of light and heat, the higher work of organic creation is carried forward. The gaseous, the liquid and the solid states of matter all wait upon the electromagnetic elements of light and heat for their beginning and permanency of structure.

The dream of our ablest philosophers, "that light and heat in the sun are generated by resistance to gravity," here finds an interpreter that teaches that *resisted gravity is light and heat* wherever it is revealed, either in sun, stars or planets.

But light and heat thus evolved are building forces, lifting matter across the dividing line between matter in space and matter in body, and then at once surrendering their burdens to cohesive affinities.

Gravital energy does its work as light and heat around the centers where resistance converts lines of gravity into glowing atoms of creative energy prepared for the joint embrace of soil and atmosphere in their nurture of seed, leaf, bud and blossom up to their perfected growths.

The work of building in all living growing forms of organic matter is carried forward by evenly balanced attractions and repulsions. The law of the falling weight and of the lifting weight is the law of gravity; above and below a common equatorial plane or center of rest the burdened currents flow, while along this plane they are deprived of their strength and deposit their burdens.

We can readily see that the flow of the positive and negative currents from the battery plates through the freely conducting wires at their immense velocity, move under the power of attractions as falling weights descend toward the earth; as they meet with resistance they are dashed into a glow of light and heat as a rapidly falling meteor, meeting with the resistance of the atmosphere, is kindled into a flame. Their like behavior in encountering resistance demonstrates the materiality of electric currents and we leave it for Prof. Tyndall to elucidate our position with one of his beautiful experiments found on page 58 of "Heat as a Mode of Motion." He says, after dealing with the question of gravital light and heat in the sun evolved from falling meteoric matter upon the body of the sun. "Let me now pass from the sun to something less, in fact, to the opposite pole of Nature. And here that divine power of the human intellect which annihilates mere magnitude in its dealings with *law*, comes conspicuously into play. Our reasoning applies not only to suns and planets, but equally so to the very ultimate atoms of which matter is composed.

"A diamond is pure carbon, and carbon burns in oxygen. I have here a diamond held fast in a loop of platinum wire; I will heat the gem to redness in this flame, and then plunge it into this jar which contains oxygen gas. See how it brightens on entering the jar of oxygen, and now it glows like a terrestrial star with a pure white light. How are we to figure the action here going on? Exactly as you would present to your minds the conception of meteorites showering down upon the sun. The conceptions are, in quality the same, and to the intellect the one is not more difficult than the other. You are to figure the atoms of oxygen showering against this diamond on all sides. They are urged towards it by what is called chemical affinity, but this force, made clear, presents itself to the mind as pure attraction, of the same mechanical quality, if I may use the term, as gravity.

"Every oxygen atom as it strikes the surface, and has its motion of translation destroyed by its collision with carbon, assumes the motion which we call heat; and this heat is so intense, the attractions exerted at these molecular distances are so mighty that the crystal is kept whitehot, and the compound, formed by the union of its atoms with those of the oxygen, flies away as carbonic acid gas."

I have here given the experiment with the explanation of the experimenter, though given to represent the theory of an incandescent sun drawing to himself cosmical matter in a solid state, and having multiplied its power by gravital velocity becomes incandescent and radiates its light and heat as sun energy back into space, a theory which makes the sun, which it claims is the sole cause of light and heat, depend upon solid cosmical matter for its support multiplied by gravital energy which the sun is supposed to impart to the descending mass, and which it seems desirable to note *in contrast* with the teachings of the electro-magnet which is our guide in our search after the true source of light and heat.

The currents of the battery and of the magnet appear to us as elements of matter moving under the power of gravital energy which appear as light and heat when dashed against resisting bodies of matter causing a mingling of their broken elements in cohesive chemical unions in space. It is thus that the light and heat of creation are evolved in the grand process of world building and also in the development of all forms of organic life from matter. And here comes in that wonderful law of gravital motion that *"resistance awakens or increases power."*

It is to this end we desired the testimony of the great experimenter that the gravital lines of energy dashed upon the sun laden with elements of matter through resistance appear as light and heat upon the surface of the sun. Granting this in the case of the diamond and it is granted as the law of sunlight, earth-light, and leads us to an acquaintance with light and heat from which we have heretofore been shut out.

The diamond experiment succeeded finely in the hands of the professor, for he had a flame in which to heat his diamond. Let him show how the sun became a heated, molten body and hence a radiator of heat and at the same time holding all the planets to their paths from his attracting gravital energy and then the whole solar system would become as luminous as the heated diamond in oxygen gas.

The power of electrical and magnetic currents as developed in the electro-magnet is too well understood to need further elucidation.

These currents we have also noticed are gathered to the magnet from surrounding space indicating a polarizing energy present with all forms of matter.

CHAPTER XIV.

LIGHT AS BUILDER.

IT NOW remains for us to follow with thought the elements of matter into which the falling currents are broken when arrested by resistants in their paths of motion. We have seen how light and heat are evolved, from what they are evolved, and we now ask what they become in the evolution?

And first we find them repellent forces. They come to the cognizance of our senses as the recoil from arrested motion of elementary atoms of matter, each atom charged with repulsive energy or lifting power equal to the velocity of its fall. It comes into place as a falling weight, and exerts its new power as a repelling energy. As such, all forms of life and motion take it in and partake of its power of exaltation.

The light has in it a magazine of power able to lift all falling weights to the plane from which they have fallen, to endow with creative energy every agency that has work to do in the great field of material progression. Light illuminates the high plane of atomic generative embrace. It marks the initial points where all life germs begin to put on the wrappings of material form, and it holds in the evenly poised balances of its omnipotence the daily strength of every thing that has life. It is also wedded to the co-ordinating power of attraction from which it cannot be separated. As light and heat appear as the results of gravital concussion receiving their lifting energy from atoms of matter resisted in their radial fall under the power of attraction, so they perform their impulsive work in a single track and in turn come again under the cold dark power of attraction. The electric spark marks with its light the period of its strength, so the illuminating and warming ray of the sunbeam is but a passing radiance. Its illuminating lines pass from darkness to darkness again at the rate of 180,000 miles in each second of time. By this circle of lifting and falling energy held in equilibrium of strength and motion by gravital centers and planes of rest all mechanical power is evolved and all creative work is done in the entire universe of matter and force. Thus the material energy of the "somewhere" comes through the constantly swinging gates of light and heat, laden with the "somewhat" from which springs into form and place all things that have life and all conditions of matter that are necessary to sustain and perpetuate life.

It is the light that reveals to us the vibrating lines of material form that we have regarded as constituting the great currents of space, and that are primary to all aggregations of matter; hence we by no means shrink from the thought that the gravital floods that are poured upon the great bodies of matter by attraction, and that are lifted radiant with the light of repulsion, thereby liberate or surrender those elementary gases and metallic elements that are built by chemical affinities into material organic structures.

The fact that chemical affinities are all under the control of electrical energy, and atoms enter into molecular unions from opposite electrical states, teaches that the sources of supply are from electro-magnetic currents.

It is well understood that atomic strength is greatest in atoms when first liberated from former unions. They are in the language of the chemist in a nascent state.

A rapid change of state of the elements of matter causes those rapid vibrations that report themselves to our senses as light and heat. By this change of state the elements are prepared to enter into the organic structures of all growing forms of being, and they are built into such forms by the working energy of the sunbeam.

Prof. Draper, of New York, has devoted a chapter in his scientific memoirs to the inquiry "of the force included in planets." He has carried forward his work under the inquiry, Whence has the force that manifests itself as heat and light in a flame been derived? "The light of the flame," he says, "is derived from particles of solid carbon issuing from combustible matters with which the wick, or gas jet is fed; these solid particles, passing from a low temperature to a white heat and undergoing eventually complete oxidation, escape into the atmosphere as carbonic-acid gas. It may be said without much error of such flame-giving compounds as we are here considering, that they are for the most part compounds of carbon with hydrogen. Under the form of oils and fats these combustible substances are derived directly or indirectly from the vegetable world." Thus in the mind of Dr. Draper, the light and heat that warm and illuminate our dwellings and the light of the sun's rays are the same; for after a series of experiments with growing plants in which he shows conclusively that without the direct action of the sun there is no absorption of growing strength to the plant, he says, "Force cannot be created, it cannot spring spontaneously out of nothing.

"The answer is, it came from THE SUN."

This is his emphatic answer concerning both the flame consuming plant structures, and the force of the flame that builds them. It is a sun-force. Again he says, "When we read by gas or by the rays of a petroleum lamp, the light we use was derived from the sun perhaps millions of years ago. The plants of those ancient days, acting as plants do now under the influence of sunshine, separate carbon from the carbonic acid of the atmosphere by associating it with the radiant energy they had absorbed, and this remained for an indefinite time enclosed, as it were, in the now combustible material, ready to be disengaged as soon as the reverse action, oxidation, takes place, returning them to commingle as heat with the active forces of the world. Much of what has here been said applies to hydrogen as well as carbon. Hydrogen is derived, under similar conditions, from the decomposition of water or ammonia. When its oxidation recurs it delivers up, under the form of heat, the energy it had absorbed." Page 187 of Memoirs.

Now, while the experiments reported in confirmation of the above statements are of the highest importance in the guidance of thought to the source of that energy that appears in the growing plant, and that is stored up in the wood and coal of our forests and mountains, at the same time the reasoning seems to fail in leading to conclusions that satisfy inquiry. Carbon and oxygen are here referred to as "flame-giving compounds;" the former, he teaches, is derived from the atmosphere, the latter from ammonia or water. We press the inquiry a step farther back of the atmosphere and back of ammonia and water and ask, whence came the carbon and the hydrogen of these compounds? And if it should be answered, they came from the sun, then we press the inquiry a step farther back and ask, from whence came the sun ? To this Prof. Draper answers, "he is the issue of nebular condensation." This answer suggests two more steps backward to the "beginning" and we inquire, whence came the nebula? and whence the power of condensation?

We suggest that condensation is gravital attraction, and gravital attraction causes matter to move on radial lines towards a gravital center ; but with the power of attraction the balancing power of repulsion always appears. This power impels matter always at right angles to radial lines, and hence nebular condensation must have been carried forward under the care of the balancing energies of attraction and repulsion. These two correlate forces must have held under control nebulous matter or elements of matter as they now hold under control the great globes of the solar system. Prof. Draper has made a distinction in his Memoir between the energy of the sun and the elements of the atmosphere that he has designated flame-giving compounds.

It seems to us that he has attempted in theory a feat

that no chemist has ever been able to perform in the laboratory, *i. e.*, to separate atoms of matter or elements of matter from the energy of matter.

The *energy* of world-building is in the atom as truly as the *material* of world-building. Cosmical matter could have had no place upon the plane of creative work without the sustaining and guiding presence of cosmical energy. There is no sun energy of greater power than carbon and hydrogen; the energy, too, of these elements of matter is in exact measure to the atoms, and they enter into combinations by atomic measures. Hence the so-called absorption of sun energy by the leaves of plants is simply atomic attraction. If carbon is thus gathered in the leaves and taken into the circulation of the sap and deposited in the growing structure of the plant by the sunlight, may we not affirm that it is carbon from the sunlight, which Dr. Draper teaches is the principal element in the "flame-giving compound" that is thus taken into the circulation of the plant, and not carbon from the atmosphere.

We deem it of the first importance that we make no error here as to the source of those atoms that are built into carboniferous structures of matter.

Both the light of the sun and the atmosphere are necessary to plant life, but which is the sovereign builder holding all of the conditions of life within its structure? The atmosphere is simply a mixture of two gases—the one a burden bearer and the other one of the most active agencies in Nature, but in it there is no place for an agency of such wonderful power, and so marked in character as either carbon or hydrogen. A trace of carbonic acid is found in the atmosphere also of ammonia; but even these may well be regarded as simply atmospheric impurities. There is no store of carbon in the atmosphere in any respect equal to the demands of plant structure.

Again the oxygen of the atmosphere only has an affinity for carbon when heated, and then, as in the glowing flame of combustion or in the building flame of the sun, oxygen comes to the carbon to aid either in its release from, or building into structure and when the carbon and oxygen unite forming carbonic acid the compound is one and one-half times heavier than common air and consequently falls to the earth as valueless to growing structures as it is destructive of animal life. It is not easy for us to see how this heavy mixture could be lifted to the leaves of plants and trees by the sunlight, and if this difficulty be overcome a still greater one appears in the quenching power that it has over both light and heat that are necessary to plant life.

We are taught "that the assumption of a green color by a germinating plant and the decomposition of carbonic acid by it are identical events," also "that sun-energy carries on this work of decomposition." We have already quoted the authority of Dr. Draper, designating carbon and hydrogen, "flame bearing compounds." Now in the full knowledge of the fact that the leaves of plants do take in carbon when exposed to the rays of the sun, while immersed in water containing carbonic acid, we affirm that the chief supply of carbon to plants is liberated from the direct rays of the sun, the sunlight not only furnishing the energy of carbon assimilation but the building substances of assimilation.

If the sun have power to take up carbon from its companionship with oxygen, carrying it into the circulation of the plant, we ask, may he not also convey in his self-evolving flame all the substances that plant-structure demands? In short, may not the sunlight be the beginning and the end of the series of material transmutations in Nature rather than the atmosphere.

May not the conservation of atoms as well as of energy, rest in the ever balancing flame of the sunbeam? Dr. Draper says, "Plants obtain carbon from the atmosphere; it constitutes the basis of their combustible portions. Sooner or later it suffers oxidation, turns back into the condition of carbonic acid, and is diffused again into the atmosphere. There is a never-ending series of cycles through which it runs: now it is in the air, now a part of the plant, now back again in the air and the same is true as regards the energy with which it is associated. Derived from the sunbeam it lay hidden in the plant, awaiting re-oxidation; then it was delivered, escaping under the form of heat or light, and remingling with the universal cosmic force from which it had been of old derived from the sun, or perhaps more correctly speaking, the sun himself was derived." Page 188-9.

Here we find a distinction clearly drawn between carbon and sun energy, or cosmic force. The cycle of carbon is from the carbonic acid of the air to the carbon of the plant and back again into the carbonic acid of the air; this gives the swing of carbon in plants from oxygen to oxygen; while "the energy with which it is associated" has a cycle from the sun to the plant; "where awaiting re-oxidation it is delivered, escaping under the form of heat or light," "remingling with the universal cosmic force;" here, the swing of cosmic energy is from space through the sun to the plant and back again under the form of light and heat to cosmic force. By carefully analyzing these so-called cycles of matter and energy as separate from each other, we find carbon primarily in the possession of oxygen, from which it is liberated by sun energy and built into the plant, from which it is delivered by re-oxidation, thus liberating the sun energy in the form of light or heat, while it is again held in the possession of oxygen, and held in the air as carbonic acid ready for a new transmutation.

Without raising the inquiry here, From whence oxygen and carbon, if not from sunlight, we ask: Whence the *energy* of oxygen and carbon that hold them in the molecular condition of carbonic acid if not from the sun? Again, how can the subordinate energy of oxygen liberate from the plant sun-energy that is the commanding cosmic force that takes on in its working power over matter the form of light and heat? Again it may be that carbon and hydrogen, which we have already learned are chief elements in a "flame-giving compound," command oxygen and are sovereign elements so that they lead the cycle of material transformations from the sun-flame of building to the oxidizing flame of combustion, and there the cycle is complete from cosmic energy and atoms of space through the sunlight to plant-forms and from plant-forms back through the flame of combustion to cosmic conditions of space.

CHAPTER XV.

SCIENTIFIC REVELATIONS.

A NEW era in scientific discovery had its beginning with Copernicus less than four hundred years ago. This philosopher announced an hypothesis of planetary motion that was not only opposed to the teaching of philosophers but was also opposed to the teachings of religion and in seeming opposition to the testimony of the senses.

The spherical form of the earth, its revolution upon its axis in about twenty-four hours of time and its revolution around the sun in each year of three hundred and sixty-five days were too wonderful to gain the belief of the people of that age who had been reared to an unquestioning faith in miracles wrought by special divine interposition in direct opposition to the well known order of Nature's laws.

To those who knew nothing of the western hemisphere, or of the boundaries of the seas, oceans and continents of the earth. the teaching of Copernicus respecting the form and velocities of the earth in its daily and annual revolutions in its path around the sun, was more difficult of belief than all the miraculous teachings of the preceding ages. A new heaven and a new earth were opened up to discovery and the old heaven and the old earth as they had viewed them, must pass away and give place to the new, or the new philosophy must be disproved.

It is no wonder that the man who had gained the first

conception of the solar system as it now stands revealed to scientific thought, should withhold his book revealing his discoveries for a third of a century. Such men are the true divine prophets of the past—the seers of the ages, and in their day are counted as profane by those who cling to the traditions of the past. Men like Copernicus, Kepler and Newton confer rich blessings upon the coming ages though they live as the rejected infidel dreamers of their own age, while their disciples in turn become scoffers at the discoverers of new truths. Thus the advanced thinkers in science find each age prepared to reject new discoveries that conflict with the reputed wisdom of the schools founded upon the teachings of the old masters.

The steps of progress that have been taken in science under the new era of discovery led by Copernicus, succeeded by Galileo, Kepler, Newton, Franklin, Galvani, Faraday, Œrestead and others have each opened new fields of thought that are sweeping away many false hypotheses of scientific thinkers and still give promise of new discoveries more wonderful than those of the past.

The tendency of all new discoveries is to simplify scientific teachings and unify the forces and facts that experimental science is constantly disclosing. The Copernican system of astronomy impressed Kepler with the thought that the motion of the heavenly bodies in space was governed by some universal law, that could be reduced to the exactness of mathematical formulas, and he sought to verify his thought by nineteen years of constant study and observation, and was rewarded by the discovery of the three great laws of planetary motion :

1. Every planet revolves in an eliptical orbit about the sun, which occupies one of the foci of such orbit.

2. The velocity of the planet in every point of its orbit is such that a line drawn from the center of the sun to the center of the planet will sweep over equal areas in equal times.

3. The square of the times of revolution of each planet, divided by the cube of its mean distance from the sun, will give a like quotient for all the planets.

The discovery of these three laws, confirmed by mathematical demonstrations the hypothesis of Kepler, that all of the motions of the planets in space are firmly held under the control of one universal law of motion. The same conviction of the great law of motion, led the mind of Newton to the discovery of the law of universal gravitation, *viz.*, The force with which two material particles respectively attract each other, is directly proportioned to their masses, and inversely proportioned to the square of the distances between their centers.

This discovery revealed the energy of planetary motion as *residing in the atoms* of matter that constitute the mass of the planetary bodies complemented by the electromagnetic currents that bear them along fixed orbital paths around fixed centers in free space. The reader may here note, that as this law of Sir Isaac Newton discloses the law governing the energy of the atom as truly as the energy of planetary bodies in their paths of motion, it follows that all molecular work in chemical unions and attractions that bind matter together in organic structures, and that give weight or power to falling bodies, together with molecular repulsions of atoms that are consequent upon the oxidation, combustion or volatilization of matter, and which produce the mechanical powers applied to the driving a water wheel, a steam engine, or a galvanic battery, must be referred to attraction of gravitation alone as the source of their power. In other words, all power of motion in matter consists of that universal energy of attraction and repulsion that is inherent in the primary atoms of which all bodies of matter are created. Hence, the scientist is brought face to face with the atoms of the sixty-three or more substances that are built into world structures as the real workers in all departments of creative work that belong to world building. Universal power is self-resident in the material form of the atom, while universal work consists in self-guided atomic unions or affinities. These thoughts lead us to the contemplation of foundation elements of all world-building, that are unseen, imponderable, immeasureable and eternal. The fact that bodies of matter attract directly as mass, has led philosophers to treat of the law of planetary motion as the law of universal attraction of gravitation, losing sight of the insensible repellent energy of matter in the planetary body, and the space through which it moves, that gives it its revolutionary velocity, constituting the equation of forces that marks out the path of the planet around the sun.

For a like reason we find the experimental work of scientific research occupied chiefly with the phenomena of matter in mass. It consists largely in weighing, measuring, dividing and mingling matter, having sensible proportions arising from the energy of attraction. Matter reduced to its primary atoms under the extreme energy of repulsion, becomes occult, and the energy that is in it works secretly and even silently; hence, our teachers of science treat of matter in only three states—the solid, the liquid and the gaseous. Over these three states attraction preponderates over repulsion and submits to exact quantitive measures. A state of matter above the gaseous reaches into the unknown and can only be reached by hypothetical reasoning, based upon the traces of its presence and power over matter in the three quantitive states. A correct hypothesis respecting matter in a fourth state may be gained from careful observation of material phenomena, that can only be accounted for by the working presence of matter outside of the three states of matter. Such hypotheses may be verified by mathematical diagrams and demonstrations. *e. g.*, The elliptical orbits of the planets were discovered by Kepler, after having spent much time and observation in attempting to verify the hypothesis that such orbits were true circles. He found the calculated places of the planets upon the theory of circles did not agree with the actual places that planets occupied in their orbits of motion.

But when he assumed the theory of the ellipticity of their orbits, both observation and mathematical calculations agreed, and the elements of the orbits of the planets thus became actually known. So, also, his hypothesis of an exact uniformity between the time periods of the revolutions of planets around the sun, and their distances from the sun, was verified in the discovery of his third law of motion, as stated on page 168. Again, Sir Isaac Newton's theory of the great law of gravity as a universal law, governing the order and periods of planetary motion, while it also caused matter to have weight determining its descent towards the center of the earth, remained for years as a mere theory, impossible of demonstration until a correct distance of the earth from the sun was obtained, and then demonstration established the correctness of his theory. In this case the theory of the philosopher was more correct than the mathematical measurements of planetary distances from the sun.

Again, in the science of chemistry there is a theory of atomic measures that gives mathematical formulas according to which atoms of matter, of which chemists can gain no actual knowledge, are united together in the formation of all chemical unions under the rigid law of atomic affinities.

Thus they find, *all ponderable combinations of matter are built up from, and by the unseen and imponderable.* In the formation of water, two gases, oxygen and hydrogen, unite in the proportion of eight parts oxygen to one part of hydrogen; *i. e.* nine pounds of water contains eight pounds of oxygen and one pound of hydrogen. These gases, the scales of the chemist may mete out, but there is demanded the energy of an electric shock to form the union, and this third element of power converts the union of the two gases into a new body, having none of the tests of their gaseous conditions. In this chemical union there is revealed the presence of a creative agency in matter that comes from the unseen and imponderable atomic form of matter that is not included in matter in its three states. From this simple formula, according to which the waters of the great oceans are built, we learn that they are created from and by the unseen and imponderable, and yet they come from material conditions and potencies of matter under the guidance of a self-determining efficiency that knows nothing of modification or change in the order and measure of their creation. Again the salt held in solution in the waters of the ocean and that becomes crystalized into cubes of rocky structure, is formed from the union of the metal sodium with the powerful bleaching agency called chlorine. These substances unite in the proportions of 23 parts sodium to 35.5 chlorine, and which are powerful destructive agents when taken separately, but when united become a necessary substance in the preparation of our food. Here too, the presence of an electrical energy presides over the union of the sodium and the chlorine, creating a new form of matter or a new substance. Electro-positive sodium, and electro-negative chlorine, unite by selective affinities according to the great law of all electro-magnetic energy, namely, unlike elements attract while like elements repel.

Again, the chlorine of salt has a strong elective affinity for the hydrogen of water, which is the cause of gathering the great bodies of water, causing the oceans, into the same groupings of materials, hence we have one of the two great divisions of earth and stone structure. The hostility of the elements thus combined in the waters of the oceans to animal and vegetable life as found upon the continents, retarded land formations, and is doubtless the chief cause of the deep depressions and low levels that constitute the great natural reservoirs of the waters of the vast oceans. Chemistry thus gives us the formula of Nature, rigidly observed in the formation of that form of matter denominated by our philosophers the second, or liquid state. Three gases, oxygen, hydrogen and chlorine, and one metal, sodium, two of the elements, sodium and hydrogen, being electro-positive, and two, oxygen and chlorine, electro-negative, bound together by natural elective affinities make the salt waters of the ocean, and these elements thus bound together cover two-thirds of the surface of the earth.

By like rigid formulas, and in like order the solid state of matter is formed. In the building of the continents the dominating element or substance is carbon in some of its protean forms. We become familiar with this substance in charcoal, mineral coal, plumbago and the diamond. Carbon is necessary to both animal and vegetable life. "It is one of the most abundant substances in Nature, forming nearly one-half of the entire vegetable kingdom, and being a prominent constituent of limestone, corals, marble and magnesian rocks." Carbon is an electro-positive element and has, at a high temperature, a strong affinity for oxygen. It performs its work in creation and in the destruction of organic substances supported by that great working agent, oxygen, at an elevated temperature, and at the same time its atoms resist the destroying power of the intensest heat. It is indestructible in the heat of combustion, while in its union with hydrogen and oxygen, the cells of plants are built up in the radial heat of the sunbeam, thereby storing up inflammable compounds that are easily consumed in the lighting and heating of our dwellings and in creating the strong blasts of furnaces used for the reduction of the ores of metals, and also in creating heat in the glowing furnaces of engines of power.

Without this wonderful element of plant-life, animal-life, and of large portions of rock structures, the continents could not have been built. In fact, without carbon the light and heat of the sunbeam, and the elevated temperature promotive of organic life would be impossible.

But the chemist finds that even this sovereign element of creative power unites with other elements in accordance with exact mathematical formulas that are ever the same. "Neither in the growing plant, animal, or rock, or in the wildest conflagration" is there a departure from the fixed law of atomic formulas of combination or dissociation. And it is worthy of notice, that all elements entering into organic life-structures, observe the same law of electro-magnetic affinities that we have already noticed in lower combinations of elements. We suggest that we do well to here raise the inquiry, though we can give no answer, whether there be not a law of a dual energy inherent in the elements of earth-building that presides over and commands all creative work?

In every chemical formula representing the creating of quantitive matter we discover that the elements and energy that build up the solids and liquids of matter though imponderable and unseen, observe rigidly the order of mathematical quantitive measures.

The formulas of Kepler and Newton that have given to

science the mathematical equations of energy and motion derived from the distances of the planets from the sun, their time periods of revolution, etc., give also the conception of a universal law of gravital attractions and repulsions that is so fixed in its order of work as to disclose to the astronomer accurate data, from which he reduces planetary motions to the unchanging verities of mathematical problems. In other words, mathematical numbers and the law of gravitation hold the same relation to each other that numbers do to quantities of sensible measure. There is, therefore, in the problems of the astronomer firmly established a highway of thought along which he can press the line of his discoveries with unerring certainty into the *material* presence of the unseen and imponderable.

Let us make the effort to trace lines of material measure across the gulf that lies between matter and material energy, in their ponderable and imponderable states between matter under the predominating power of attraction, and matter under the dissociate state of repulsion.

The order which we have noted in the chemical unions of some of the elements of matter has given us the conception of atoms and energy as the first things of solid and liquid matter.

These first things are so real to the chemist that he definitely notes their presence in the changes of the states of substances, and designates the exact order of their work, and yet they have their home in forms so infinitesimal that they elude the search of microscopic glasses, or the touch of the most delicate organs of sense.

Says Balfour Stewart ''a simple elementary atom is

truly an immortal being, and enjoys the privilege of remaining unaltered and essentially unaffected amid the most powerful blows that can be dealt against it; it is probably in a state of ceaseless activity and change of form, but it is nevertheless always the same. In this ceaseless activity there is a barrier to an intimate acquaintance with molecules and atoms, for even if we could see them they would not remain at rest sufficiently long to enable us to scrutinize them. Could we see an atom, and could we illuminate it by a flash of electricity, the atom would most probably have vibrated many times during the exceedingly small time of the flash. In fine, the limits placed upon our senses, with respect to space and time, equally preclude the possibility of our ever becoming directly acquainted with these exceedingly minute bodies, which are nevertheless the raw materials of which the whole universe is built.''

It is readily seen that when we try to analyze matter and resolve it into its elements that we are at once guided into the presence of first forms of matter and first acts of energy that make all things of creation, *certain and possible.*

They are grand sovereign potencies and sovereign forms that work all things according to identity of being and elective affinities that have been with them from the first gathering of atoms in space under the great law of attraction of gravitation.

Matter could never have been gathered under any other law. The rocky foundations of the earth could not have been laid, the ocean beds prepared and their vast bodies of water gathered, the continents could not have been lifted out of the waters, covered with lakes and rivers, with mountains and plains, with forests and verdure-clothed fields; and above all, the infinite forms of animal life that are fed upon earth's teeming harvests, without the established order of atomic attractions that we have imperfectly sketched.

The atoms of matter that Balfour Stewart has styled "immortal, and the raw materials of which the universe is built," by the living force that is in them, give substance and form to all of the varied combinations of matter into which they enter, as truly as the seed gives character to the plant-form that is unfolded from it.

We have found that each formula of chemical unions establishes an equation of both force and atomic numbers.

Each atom has within itself a dual energy of attraction and repulsion, or of choosing and rejecting; but at the same time all are not endowed with a like energy. They are divided equally according to electro-magnetic law, so that atoms charged with opposite polarities are alone united in stable compounds or chemical affinities. The raw material then, out of which the universe is built is equally divided in its elementary conditions, and it is certain that the conditions of the atoms are impressed upon the organic unions into which atoms are built, under their selective affinities. This leads us to the acceptance of Sir Isaac Newton's law of universal gravitation in its fullest and broadest sense, so that all forms of matter are built up under the constant working energy of the electro-magnetic forces. If the question be here raised as to the whence of matter and of creative energy, we find the answer at our hand, and say, *They came from the great magnetic sea of balanced forces, in which the suns and planets constituting all worlds are balanced upon accurately poised centers of equal attractions and repulsions.*

Of the nature of this sea of forces, we may perhaps learn more than we have heretofore thought possible. It is a sea as boundless as space and pervaded by lines of metallic form or currents of virgin matter that compass space with their vibrating energy.

Professor Crooks, of England, by experimenting with direct reference to an acquaintance with the condition of space when deprived of the presence of air or the gases, under the exhausted bell glass of an air pump, has made the experimental discovery of what he calls the fourth state of matter. He says, "So distinct are the phenomena of this experiment from anything that occurred in air or gas at the ordinary tension, that he was led to assume that we were here brought face to face with matter in a fourth state or condition,—a condition as far removed from the state of gas as gas was from the liquid. In some of its properties radiant matter was as material as wood or iron, while in other properties it almost assumed the character of radiant energy. We had touched the border-land where matter and force seem to merge into each other,—the shadowy realm between the known and the unknown." He ventured to think "that the greatest scientific problems of the future would find their solution in this border-land and even beyond, where, it seemed to him, lay ultimate realities, subtle, far-reaching and wonderful."

Let the thought of Mr. Crooks be here grasped, that radiant matter and radiant energy have their home in space and then we learn that the great sources of creative organic power and form flow from space to body, and hence each revolving sun or planet gathers power and atomic matter from its field of motion according to its gravital strength of attraction.

Radiant matter, so far as planetary bodies are concerned is not in any case wasting energy and wasting matter such as is witnessed under a devouring flame, but on the other hand it is the radiant matter of space under the strong gravital attraction of planetary bodies, and is drawn with the velocity of light on radial lines toward the centers of such bodies, and through atmospheric resistance becomes light and heat in glowing lines of gravital energy. These radiant lines of energy and matter are attacked by oxygen, torn asunder and broken into atomic forms that seek rest upon the heated body of the planet according to the already noticed law of selective affinity. For it is to be remembered that we regard the radiant state of matter of Prof. Crooks as Balfour Stewart's raw material out of which the solids, liquids and gases of matter are formed. The reader is referred to a more full statement and elucidation of our thought in another part of this work.

And now let us pass to a careful study of space filled with radiant matter and radiant energy and see if we have not already attained a better acquaintance with the state of matter in space than we have supposed. The thought that we have already reached is that of material universal unity. The laws of Kepler teach it. The law of universal gravitation teaches it. The electro-positive and electro-negative states of atoms teach it. The exact quantitive formulas of the chemist according to which all bodies of matter are created teach it. The uniformity of light from all worlds and in all ages confirms it.

CHAPTER XVI.

THE UNSEEN WORLD.

THE unity of matter and the unity of force to the student of Nature elude discovery in an unseen land, while it is in vision sought for as a revelation from a land of promise.

As we have seen in a former chapter that all forms of matter are organized out of invisible atoms and by invisible forces, and yet according to rigid mathematical formulas, and as the same formulas will remain the same in all lands, so we may conclude they have been the same in all ages. This insight into the methods of Nature in organization, carries thought back to the beginnings of creation, and also reveals the same agencies and elements around us in space that have been bound together in the foundations upon which the heavens and the earth have been reared. Without the elements and energy of space there could be no solid land, no waters for rivers or oceans, and no atmosphere or light, making life possible.

This being so, we gain acquaintance with all states of matter, and every form of energy, and all sources of power, by the careful study of our own environment. The radiant energy and the radiant matter that come to the philosopher in his experimental work, come to all philosophers in all places upon the earth, and to all thinking beings in all worlds.

The planets sweep through space at immense velocities, our own earth moving at the rate of a thousand miles in each minute of time, compassing a circuit of 552,000,000 of miles in a single year, and yet in all the long journey there come to us no new experiences denoting a change of environment, and to the earth there has come no new revelations in space in the ages past, and there can come none in the circles of the eternities to come. The light of the sunbeam has been an object of study for the philosophers of all ages, and it has always appeared as radiant energy, and now we are beginning to learn that it is also radiant matter. It takes but one more step of thoughtful inquiry to gain the conviction that the radiance of the sunbeam is simply an illumination of the radiant matter of the space around us in which we live and move and from which has come our life and being.

These thoughts guide us, not only to the border-land of elementary being but they also reveal in this border-land the perennial source of all material energy, whether creative or mechanical. It must lead us also to discard the teachings of the philosophers of the past ages that the sun is the source of all power upon the earth. Sir John Herschel writes, "The sun's rays are the ultimate source of almost every motion which takes place upon the surface of the earth. By its heat are produced all winds, and those disturbances in the electric equilibrium of the atmosphere which give rise to the phenomena of lightning, and probably also to all terrestrial action and the aurora. By their vivifying action vegetables are enabled to draw support from inorganic matter, and become in their turn the support of animals and man, and the source of those great deposits of dynamical efficiency which are laid up for human use in our coal strata." Referring the reader to a more full elucidation of the philosophy of elementary material energy on "Sunlight," page 1, we desire here to simply call attention to the radiant matter of universal space as the primary source of all material power or of universal energy. The fact that the sun is the sensible expression of vast power, and that it far transcends all the planetary bodies of the solar system in manifestation of energy, does by no means teach that it is the *source* of material energy.

The law of universal attraction of gravitation according to which sun and planets are united in one system of forces, simply reveals a reciprocal exchange of energy between sun and planets. The *source* of their power must be from without and around them. The fountain of energy must be superior to the mere sensible expression of such energy.

The floods of radiant matter and radiant energy that enswathe sun and planets in their radial and orbital lines of omnipotent strength, are to these bodies the everlasting fountains from which flow through and around them all of their upholding and evolving power.

As all sensible forms of matter are built from elementary atoms, so all sensible displays of power also find their source in the same elementary forms.

Let it be noted that by radiant matter we do not have specific reference to light; as we regard light as an affection of radiant matter arising simply from a temporary elevation of temperature through resistance of the lines of radiant matter passing through a resisting medium. The radiance of illumination enables us to look in upon radiant matter as it moves in space. The radial lines of the sunbeam are independent of the light and heat that are evolved from them. Light is not a "mode of motion" but an illumination of radiant lines of elementary matter in motion. Prof. Tyndall teaches by experiment, that the dark lines above and below the sensible spectrum as diffused by the prism, have more chemical and heating power than the illuminated lines, clearly teaching that the energy called light and heat belongs to the radiant lines of space resisted in their intense velocities of motion and their temperature raised by the work done in passing the resisting medium. We may well then eliminate light and heat from the class of imponderable forces, and regard them as simply indices of force or energy. If we thus cancel out light and heat from the list of elementary or imponderable forces that science gives us, we have gravitation, mechanical force, electricity, magnetism, and chemical affinity.

For this entire list of forces we may substitute the force of attraction and repulsion that exists between the electro-positive and electro-negative states of radiant matter and we have resolved all of the different manifestations of force into the co-working polarizing forces of electricty and magnetism.

Now we have already shown by reference to the affinities of atomic forms of matter that they obey rigidly the law of magnetic attractions and repulsions in the formation of material compounds and in the growth of organic bodies, consequently we are constrained to regard all forms of matter and all varieties of living organic bodies built from electro-magnetic elements of matter into electro-magnetic forms of being.

It is therefore no marvel that the vast bodies of matter composing the great suns and sun systems of worlds should be held in perfect subjection to the polarizing forces of the magnet and that they should be so nicely balanced upon their centers of motion, that they should fly through space with such wonderful velocities, and that they should be fixed in the heavens in families bound together by indissoluble ties of gravital affinity.

We have here reached a plane of thought that enables us to take in the entire work of creation at a single glance. The beginning and the end of matter are brought into view in the completed circle of atomic work that goes on under the working energy of the so-called sunbeam from seed-time to harvest and from the harvest to the dying seed, giving promise of a second harvest. Radiant matter is drawn on radial lines to the center of the perfected seed passing through the resisting atmosphere and earth, that both warm and dissociate the lines of radiance into atoms which under the law of affinity are built silently in unerring order into the evolving structure of the plant. Here the order of organic work in matter is from the extreme of repulsion through magnetic attractions drawing matter atom by atom to its true place in the growing organism. Through this same order all of matter in all worlds has passed under the guidance of the great law of universal gravitation from environing space toward fixed centers of growing strength, evolving all the grand results of life, form and motion. "As it was in the beginning" so it is now and so will it ever remain. The order of the work will never change; the even balance between attraction and repulsion will never be disturbed. The energy of all bodies of matter is measured by inherent energy of the atoms composing them and they are environed in a sea of radiant or repellent matter of equal strength to their strength of attraction measured by atomic units of strength.

CHAPTER XVII.

LATENT AND SENSIBLE POWER.

THE new hypothesis that we have ventured to oppose to the teachings of science respecting the sources of material energy, devolves upon us the necessity of indicating the scientific boundary line between latent and sensible power, or between latent and sensible heat. Our hypothesis compels us to discover this boundary line in the intercommunion of the attracting and repellent dual energy of radiant matter. It will be an easy matter for the reader to accept the thought that the attracting and repelling energy of the opposite poles of a magnet reveal the simplest sources of power that we find· in matter. The peculiarity of the magnet, as a source of power, is, that it gathers its strength from its immediate environment, drawing from a source of power that is universal and eternal. Both conditions of power are here found in a bar of hardened steel, *i. e.*, attraction and repulsion. These polar forces work across a neutral center of rest, revealing two equal hemispheres of radiant energy, limited by an equatorial plane of rest extended at right angles to the magnet, from its center of rest.

These hemispheres of real energy being equally balanced, can of themselves make no display of power. To reveal their strength, other bodies capable of responding to magnetic impulse must be brought into the field of their influence, and power is then revealed. But this power is the power of aggregation, drawing to the magnet, as if it were itself a unit of energy, subordinate atoms of magnetically charged matter.

Here we notice the display of power or energy, but not working power. The power of steam is a working power because the heat of the furnace has awakened in the molecules of water the power of repulsion and the temporary repellent force of the heated atoms is passed to the steam engine and drives the followers of the piston rod back and forth imparting power to working machinery.

The latent power that has been treasured up in the wood and the water under the silently working forces of magnetization, that have built up all organic forms of matter, is attacked by the disorganizing power of oxidation or combustion; the balance between the equal forces of attraction and repulsion that exists in the restful states of matter, is disturbed, and the repellent energy thus awakened imparts of its power within the resisting walls of the engine to the uses of machinery.

Here we have power from the polar force of repulsion while from the revolving water-wheel we are enabled to take power from the equal force of attraction. In both cases it is a resultant from the disturbed balance of the dual polar forces of attraction and repulsion. Latent power is the established plane of the evenly balanced and evenly working forces of the magnet. Sensible power and sensible heat arise from a temporary mechanical disturbance of these forces, lifting atomic elements of matter violently above the neutral plane of balanced polarizing forces.

Thus when we trace all forms of power to their source,

we shall find that source to be radiant energy in its two forms of radiant matter that are revealed both in the electro-magnet and in the great planetary bodies of space. Both earth and magnet find a rest-center, and both attract and repel at their northern and southern poles, a unit of force. The dream of the enthusiast that mechanical power can be evolved from the elements of matter without the use of force in some form, cannot be realized from the fact that all energy of motion tends constantly to the rest plane of equally working forces of attraction and repulsion. This fact will limit all mechanical contrivances for the generation of power, to the one question of economy in generating and utilizing it. No advantages can be taken of the immensity of power working normally in matter for the great law of polarization holds all forms of energy to a fixed plane of an even balance. The magnet is a unit of latent power, and only reveals its strength in its disturbed state from other magnets.

Again, we here learn that in the grand economy of creation, the extremes of matter in their states of attraction and repulsion are co-ordinate and fixed sources of power. From radiant matter in space to solid matter in planetary forms or from solid matter to radiant matter, the work of the creative forces is carried forward. The lowest level of latent energy or latent heat is reached at the two extremes of gravital attractions and orbital repulsions. While the summit level of light-heat and creative energy is at the surface of body, where atmospheric resistance interposes a break to the free interchange of magnetic currents laden with oppositely charged forces.

Except in these atmospheric belts upon the surface of bodies, all of matter, both solid and radiant, is cold and dark, and hence the grand sources of power are latent and unrevealed to the evolving forms of organic being. It is therefore manifestly impossible that power should be transferred from sun to earth, or from earth to sun except along the low plane of latent magnetic energy which is the lowest plane of temperature of interstellar space. A high state of temperature at the surface of the sun could have no possible effect upon the planets in shedding upon them light and heat, as Nature stores up her power in the latent and silent flow of the balanced polarizing forces of gravital energy.

It is not possible to store up power at any temperature above the temperature of radiant energy, in its equally balanced and silently working lines of gravital attractions and gravital energy; and we have seen that gravital, radiant elementary matter works at the low temperature of the darkness of stellar space.

The attraction of gravitation holds within its radiant floods, all of power adjusted to an equal balance, while it controls all of the grand revolutions and infinite velocities of matter in space. In its complete working unity it meets with no resistance, and consequently works throughout the entire universe at a low, even temperature. It works at the lowest possible level of latent power, or latent heat in matter. Hence, the grand velocities of radiant matter and of planetary bodies in space create no more disturbance from resistance than though they were at rest. The light and heat of the sun and planets arise from local disturbances of gravital attractions, confined to the atmospheric envelope surrounding them, and they maintain their power and brightness from a constant atmospheric disturbance arising from the uniform presence of the atmosphere enveloping them. Hence, the light and heat of sun and planets are a constant quantity, because they are generated by a constant gravital power passing through a constantly resisting medium. The light of the sun would be quenched at once if the resisting atmospheric medium of the sun's environment could be instantly removed. In like manner would the light of the sun be put out if the sun's body should lose his low temperature of latent energy at which we have seen all gravital forces perform their constant work. Again, the sun cannot lose heat by radiation because it is generated by his own power of attraction, and consequently must hold all wasting or evolved elements from light or heat within his own grasp of power. As well might water flow up the sides of mountains, or stones and rocks be lifted into space as the mists of the ocean are lifted, as that the light and heat of the sun should be radiated millions of miles across free space to the planets; or in other words, that power generated in the form of light and heat on the body of the sun should be transferred to the planets as light and heat by radiation.

There are but two forces that control the changes of matter; one is the force of attraction, or aggregation; the other is the force of repulsion, or diffusion. In free space these forces constitute the compound force of planetary motion. Under the combined influence of these forces attraction increases as the planet nears the sun's body, and repulsion is correspondingly increased to preserve a balance of orbital motion. Hence, the planets as they approach the sun have their velocity increased, and as they recede their velocity is diminished.

Now, heat upon the surface of the sun is local repellent energy exerted or awakened at the expense of the local attracting energy of the sun's body, if it be the heat of combustion; but the vast attracting energy of the sun that is equal to the centrifugal energy that drives the planets in their orbits must be immensely greater than the local repellent energy that may be awakened in the sun's photosphere; consequently, the radiation of such matter as might be disturbed by local combustion on the surface of the sun would be neutralized and quenched by attraction at but an inconsiderable distance from the sun's body.

The economy of the great forces of material creation is such that local attractions are always equal to local combustions.

The low temperature at which universal gravitation exerts its power is the plane of conservation of force, and must ever preserve the universe from the over mastery of either one of the correlate forces of universal power. The universe of matter can neither "melt with fervent heat," nor "be rolled together like a scroll," so long as the cold dark, silently working forces of gravitation maintain their power over matter.

By reviewing our position it will be seen that we regard light and heat as sensible displays of power arising from local disturbances of the balance that Nature persistently maintains between the two polar forces of gravital attraction and repulsion. These forces undisturbed, or unresisted, work silently and evenly, like a rapidly revolving wheel that is evenly centered and balanced. The wonderful power of motion in matter is latent because insensible. Resistance to this power awakens sensible displays of power equal to the power of resistance. It requires a constant resistant to give a constant sensible power. The sensible power will be determined by the power of resistance and at the local points of resistance. Temporary resistance will give only temporary sensible power, and such power will only be equal to the supply of resisting elements. Heat and light are to us sensible measures of either a constant or a temporary resistance to the forces of attraction and repulsion. Conservation of energy marks the limits of sensible power, always equal to the initial impulse of power imparted at the disturbing point of motion. The heat units expended in lifting a body to any distance above the earth will be restored to the body in its return to the earth. The heat applied to lifting the body is that of repulsion, the heat acquired by the falling body is restored by attraction. The first is temporary resistance, the second is the measure of such resistance.

Nothing is gained by the work thus performed, even if the falling body should do work in returning to the earth. The loss by combustion is only equivalent to the work performed by attraction. Thus the mechanical power gained by multiplying units of sensible heat by combustion is at the expense of heat stored up in some form lifted to its place above the level of latent heat by the influence of the sun. Hence our philosophers are already sounding an alarm respecting the great loss that our supplies of coal and wood are suffering from the demands made upon them to create mechanical power. Now in the sensible work performed by the heat of the sun there is a vast accumulation of power without any sensible source of waste. The wind and the waterfall are constant supplies of power capable of doing mechanical work, and they are lifted to their positions of working power by the influence of the sun on the temperature of the earth. All forms of vegetable life are also nourished by the warming energy of the sunbeam and store up in their growing organisms vast supplies of heat energy for the support of animal life and furnishing fuel sufficient to meet all of the demands of civilization, for the cooking of food, the warming of dwellings, the heating of forges and furnaces, and also supplying mechanical power for the driving of machinery.

The great problem here demanding a solution is, *how do the latent forces of gravital attraction become converted into the sensible heat of the sunbeam?*

The heat of the sun seems to come down upon the earth with the power of a descending weight, accumulating strength until it reaches the earth. Its measured velocity is 180,000 miles for each second of time. It meets upon the earth's surface a return shock of radiant energy that serves to multiply its power and carries with it rising mists and vapors that give to the winds and the waterfalls their sources of power. The law of gravity is here certainly the law of intercommunion between sun and earth, and as distance is eliminated from the problem it follows that sun and earth attract each other directly as mass, *i. e.*, the sun attracts the earth with a force measured by the attraction of the earth for the sun, as the distance between the two bodies is simply zero in the problem.

As the mutual attractions between these two bodies act upon radial lines, and as sun and earth are huge magnets, we assume that the poles of the earth are reversed to those of the sun and that the laws of magnetic attraction teach us that positive and negative polar forces flowing oppositely between sun and earth establish the bond of union between them. If this be so the transfer of energy must be equal between these two bodies and this flow must be through space at the low level of latent energy. These two oppositely moving floods of energy passing under the great law of attraction of gravitation pass through more than 90,-000,000 miles of radiant matter in eight minutes of time and enter the resisting atmosphere of sun and earth, their currents thrilling with energy at a high tension of opposite polarities to those of the revolving bodies beneath their atmospheric envelope and by this means attraction of gravitation pours a constant flood of light and heat upon both sun and planets. According to the theory of latent and sensible heat that we have thus imperfectly sketched the light and heat of the sun and the planets of the solar system evolved from their resisting atmospheres become creative potencies, deriving their vast power from their environing space of radiant matter.

According to this theory there is no solar waste, no radiating light and heat from sun to planets, while creative power is evolved at the point of time and place in which the work is done.

CHAPTER XVIII.

RADIANT MATTER AND MECHANICAL POWER.

AS we have to do with occult forces and forms of matter, great care is necessary in determining the lines of thought that acquaint us with such phenomena as teach their existence. False assumptions or false theories will hide from us the objects of our search.

The assumption of our philosophers that all of matter is comprised in three states, has restrained thought and retarded discoveries in the unseen realms of space and of matter in imponderable forms in space.

Light, heat, gravitation, mechanical force, electricity, magnetism and chemical affinity have therefore been regarded as outside of the universe of matter, while space has been regarded as vacuity, having no other relation to matter than simply affording the somewhere for its place and grand velocities.

Into this unknown realm of cold, deep darkness our senses do not lead us; to them it must ever remain as the unknown. But it is a realm out of which come all the grand facts and forces of the three sensible forms of matter. It is also the realm from whence come the wonderful phenomena of life, soul, spirit, thought, consciousness, with all the elements of mind-force, and it is the whither of all changes of matter and of all that we know of life. If there be an immortality and a realm of pure spiritual existences, they must be enswathed in matter in its immortal and radiant state. If there ever were a period when the visible worlds of space were unformed, they must have had place in space under the conditions of radiant energy and radiant matter*; at least, we venture this assumption in the line of our inquiry into the behavior of matter in its radiant state. Our acquaintance with the radiant state of matter must begin with matter in its solid state. The human mind can only commence its investigation where the great work of material creation ends. Mind in material structures finds its place in the last of the long series of the involving forms of matter.

As complaint has been made to that school of scientific thought that treats of creation as a process of *evolution*, we will heed the criticism and regard all creative work in matter as a work of *involution*. The order of work is involution, but the forms of matter that come into place from the involutionary work of material energy are the products of such work and seem evolved therefrom.

The first step we take from the solid form of matter is to matter in its liquid or flowing state, and in the liquid state of matter we commence our acquaintance with matter taking on the form of currents. In these currents we gain our first lessons respecting the mechanical power of matter. A dam is constructed across the current of a stream of water, resisting its flow; power is accumulated at this resisting barrier by the rising of the waters and such accumulated power is devoted to mechanical work.

This simple experiment is made useful to the mechanic because it furnishes him a power equal to that of many horses, for driving his machinery, and prepares the way for great improvements in the arts of civilization, by awakening inquiry respecting the actual sources of power in matter. In the adjustment of the machinery erected by the side of such a power, developed by the resistance interposed to the flowing current of a mountain stream, the mechanic takes great pains to avoid all possible friction; his wheels must be accurately centered and evenly balanced; all the journals or bearings must be freely lubricated, all possible contact of wheels, belts and pulleys with resisting substances must be avoided, because resistance not only retards motion but developes power from the repellent energy of matter that also moves in currents, adverse to those of the flowing stream.

This antagonism of friction to the working power of machinery is a factor of power that arises from the fact that all forms of sensible power arise from forcible resistance to flowing currents; such currents, either moving upward from the plane of universal gravitation, or downward toward such plane. In the flowing stream the dam is a resistant to currents flowing downward towards the lowest level of rest in the great plane of latent energy. In the friction that resists the motion of wheels and pulleys, there is a resistance that awakens currents of energy that lift currents of matter above or away from such plane.

In the experiments of Count Rumford upon the nature of frictional energy, he was enabled to boil water by means of a frictional cylinder driven by horse power, in two hours and thirty minutes. Now if such a frictional cylinder be attached to the machinery that we have supposed erected by the dam of the flowing stream, and water is boiled, then a steam engine built by the side of the water-mill could be operated by power derived from the water wheel. Then again, to this steam engine could be attached one of Mr. Edison's dynamo-electrical machines, and currents of electricity could be generated from the currents of radiant matter that flow around the poles of fixed magnets and this electrical energy led off in currents to the carbon resistants of his electric lamps, which act, in the piling up or multiplying of power, as the dam does in the flowing stream, and a brilliant display of electrical light is secured. But our circle of forces is not complete without we take into account the radiant energy of the sun's light and heat that lifted the waters of the oceans and lakes into the gathering clouds in the form of mist, and giving them to the radiant currents within the atmosphere, that are also guided by sun energy, deposited them upon the mountains and thus feeding the fountains from which the rivers flow.

It will be noticed by carefully tracing all exhibitions of power that may come under our observation that radiant matter and radiant energy are *necessary conditions* of power. All forms of power may be interposed between the radiant energy of the sunbeam and the radiant energy of the glowing flame as seen between the resisting carbons of the electric current. Liquids and solids of matter may have their place in the series but they cut no figure as primary sources of power. Hence, our scientists have been led to teach that the sun is the source of all power upon the earth. Again, I desire to notice the fact that radiant energy is inseparable from radiant forms of matter. There is need of exercising great caution here in gaining clear conceptions of radiant forms of material energy. It has been a matter of grave inquiry among philosophers whether heat is a species of matter or a species of motion. The accepted theory is, that it is a species of motion. One objection to heat as being a substance, is, that a heated body is not sensibly heavier than a cold one.

Now it should be borne in mind that weight in matter is simply local or sensible unbalanced energy. The vast bodies of matter constituting the solar system, are in relation to each other without weight because they are evenly balanced by that universal energy called attraction of gravitation, which we have coupled with universal repulsion. It requires sensible displays of power to lift a stone from the earth, because it is only lifted against the great power of unbalanced material energy. When lifted from the earth by the energy of heat, it in falling again to the earth gives off or awakens as much heat power as was required to lift it. The great balance of energy is not affected by the change of position of the stone by heat-power, but when the stone approaches the earth it has weight of energy added to its weight of matter, equal to the heat energy applied to the lifting of the stone from the earth. Thus heat finds a place among the sensible sources of power, because of its power to promote local disturbances between bodies and within bodies of matter.

If it does not add weight to bodies of matter, it is capable of reducing them to a radiant state and thus depriving them of all weight. In short, heat is the local unbalanced energy of repulsion and always appears in its power over matter as the peer of the local unbalanced energy of attraction. In the series of powers that we have grouped together by the flowing stream, we find that each class of power consists of two equal and oppositely working forces, the heat of the sun dissociates water, takes it up as radiant matter, holds it above the earth till overcome by attraction, and then pours it upon the earth supplying the waste of all of earth's flowing springs and rivers of water that are diverted to driving the wheels of mechanical power.

The radiant energy of the sun again appears in the frictional energy of the heating cylinder and this energy contends with the attracting energy of the water converting it into the repellent energy of the steam that furnishes energy to the moving piston of the engine. Now if the whole power of the water-wheel has been used in the heating of the water in the frictional cylinder for the supply of power to the steam engine there has been simply a conversion of power. No work has been done except the work of conversion. But by observing the changes in the conditions of matter in the conversion of power from that of attraction, as in the falling water, and that of repulsion as in the steam engine, we find that it changes states, passing from the solid or liquid to the radiant, or from the radiant to the solid or liquid. In its radiant state it is not only without weight, but lifts weights; in its solid state it is seemingly without power, is called dead or inert, while in its liquid state it has only the power of position that is transient like the power of a falling weight.

In this process of the conversion of matter from a solid to a radiant state we are compelled to treat the sensible impression made upon us that we call light and heat, as a sympathetic affection between our bodies and the bodies that are passing through the process of conversion.

The radiant matter surrounding the changing body is aroused, set in rapid motion, and carries on the work of taking in pieces the changing body, atom by atom, and converting it into lines of radiant matter. The radiant matter that thus does its work upon the changing body also works through our bodies, giving to them the sensation called heat, and the rapid vibrations of the radiant matter surrounding the changing body give to the eye the sensation of light. The sensation of light marks the elevated plane to which matter must be lifted in passing through a change of states, whether it be from solid to radiant or from radiant to solid. The normal temperature of radiant and solid matter is always the same, hence a change of states only occurs when both are lifted to the elevated plane of corresponding affinities, where atomic unions are temporarily released from the conservating forces of the great law of universal gravitation.

With these thoughts in mind we shall find no difficulty in regarding radiant matter as really distinct from light and heat as solid matter is. The radiant lines of the sunbeam are real lines of energy independent of the temporary illumination that reveals them. It is with this world of radiant matter that we must gain an acquaintance as a new world of philosophical research. It is really the world in which we live, rather than the world of matter in its ponderable forms. Our acquaintance can never be made with the great laws of physics in their working harmony so long as we remain in ignorance of the all pervading presence of *radiant matter* as the infinite source of material phenomena.

When the scientist finds that lines of radiant matter constitute the medium through which light comes from sun and stars and he discovers in such light the lines that the metals take on when exposed to high conditions of heat, he will then learn that he is discovering more of the metallic conditions of environing space than of the substances that are in sunlight or starlight. And if we might not overburden our theme we would here suggest that the vibrations of radiant matter not only give us sensible light and heat, but also sound. The atmosphere has heretofore borne burdens and done work from which it will be released so soon as an acquaintance is gained with radiant conditions of matter in free space. The gases also have had a part to perform that they have but slight capabilities of performing.

With these explanatory thoughts we are I trust prepared to gain a more perfect acquaintance with the third form of power in the series of powers that we have grouped together. In this form of power radiant matter appears as the chief factor of power supplied and work done.

Avoiding any detailed account of the machinery used for generating powerful electric currents for the purposes of the electric light, we only need to say that the power of the engine is applied to the work of making and breaking polar attractions between fixed and temporary magnets, producing rapidly changing magnetic impulses that induce magnetic and electrical currents from the immediate surrounding space, of immense power. The electrical currents thus induced from free space are led off to the electric burner by conducting wires, the carbon burner being a resistant in the electric current, like all other resistants to rapidly moving energies, evolves light and heat at the break where the local resistant is applied. The radiant matter of the magnets and of the conducting wires is neither light nor heat, any more than the wheels of the cars of a railroad train are, that give off both light and heat when motion is resisted by the application of the brakes; but the rapid vibrations of radiant matter raised to a high temperature in clashing against a resisting medium, as rifle balls become heated by clashing against a resisting target, report themselves to the eye and to the organs of sense as light and heat. As we have before indicated, the presence of light and heat mark the highest plane of atomic changes in which matter and energy co-work in forming living, sensitive organisms. It is the high plane of living forms and of thinking, sensitive brain power.

It also marks the plane where positive and negative currents of force are broken up into atoms of opposite affinities preparatory to combination according to the laws of magnetic affinity in sustaining life.

This elevated plane of matter we reach at the border line of ponderable matter and consequently at the line of the unseen and unknown, and yet at this meeting line of radiant matter and sensitive, organic life, we find the vanishing line of the highest working plane of material energy that can be attained in developing mechanical power.

The lowest working plane of such energy is that of magnetic attraction in body, and electrical repulsion in space. These forces, as we have seen, work at the low temperature of inter-stellar space, and we may here add with opposite polar forces and fixed centers of rest that command universal order and undisturbed harmony.

The atmosphere represents the belt of working mechanical forces as they are by Nature limited upon the earth's surface. Across this belt the mountains and valleys rise and fall as working lines of energy. They must have come into place under the repelling and attracting working energy of the mechanical couple of opposing forces. The lower line of this belt is the sea level of the silent magnetic couple of the two forces of magnetic energy that have presided over earth-planes of work, preserving the center of gravity of the earth with its spherical form and equal polar hemispheres and at the same time establishing the great equatorial plane of balanced magnetic energy. Below this line there is but one couple of forces and they work from the rest center of the earth to this line of the sea level. The couple of forces stored up within this boundary line of magnetic energy, is joined with the sun in a couple of power that gives to both sun and earth this belt of working forces displaying light and heat and promoting the formation of all living structures. The sun and earth, working over against each other in a magnetic couple, keep in play through the environing atmosphere of the two bodies the couple of forces—attraction and repulsion—that are necessary to all working mechanical powers. These two forces as we have stated work through the resisting atmosphere as resistants, developing power simultaneously upon earth and sun.

Hence, we are enabled to account for the counter flow of streams of water from the sea level to the tops of the mountains, against an atmospheric pressure of fifteen pounds to the square inch. In this work radiant matter lifts in the lines of the sunbeam to the tops of the hills and mountains with a power equal to that of all the flowing waters in their descent to the sea. Let it be distinctly noted and carefully fixed in the mind that it is not the atmosphere that does this work, but radiant lines of material energy working through the atmosphere. These lines of radiant matter carry heat, moisture, light and sound through the atmosphere, while it is constantly supplying the brake of its sluggish compound.

Even the motions of the atmosphere in direct lines of motion with its often fearful velocities, are directed by the radiant lines of energy that work through it from magnetic sources of power above and beneath it.

Our books of philosophy teach us that evaporation goes on in vacuum as freely as under the pressure of the atmosphere, and at the same time the atmosphere wrenches from the cold, dark level of universal energy, by its resistance, all of sensible power that appears in this belt of working powers that we have endeavored to visualize.

In the process of world formation, this belt that we have designated as some twelve thousand feet in depth around the earth, has been pressed constantly outward as the work of earth formation has gone forward, step by step in the progress of the ages, covering from the beginning of living structures according to the testimony of their rocky sepulcher, a distance of more than twenty miles. Within this belt as the workshop of radiant, creative forces, there is discovered the true history of creation. It is in vain, and out of the line of our present work, to attempt to compute the periods of time consumed in this work, but this we know, that ages have made no haste in their creative work, and hence twenty miles in thickness of stratified rock over the great continents of the earth must assure us of a time past that thought cannot measure. And the matter out of which these rocky structures were built, from whence did it come, if not from the radiant material energy that guides the planets in their lines of motion?

CHAPTER XIX

FROM WHENCE ROCKS.

THE line of our work has led us into an acquaintance with currents of matter flowing under the power of the grand energy of attraction toward the low sea level of ocean formation. Again, we have seen that currents of radiant matter gather a constant tribute from the great fountains of lakes and oceans, and lift the water in atomic or misty forms through the atmosphere above the continents with their lofty mountains and thus pouring out from cloudy chariots an abundant supply of rain drops, both for replenishing the fountains and refreshing all forms of life upon the earth. Under the working circles of these radiant lines of matter every species of life took on from some whence material bodily form—the growing rocks, even, took on the form of solids from low conditions of life. "The great pyramids of Egypt," we are told, "are formed of stones which owe their origin to the chalk shells of minute animals. The stones of which nearly the whole city of Paris is built consist of the shells of animals, of which two hundred millions are computed in a cubic foot." The limestone of the Trenton period was evidently an involution of matter from moluscan life. Geology teaches that the beds of Trenton limestone abound in fossils, some of them being literally made up of shells, trilobites and corals, while the surfaces of the slaty layers are frequently thickly strewn with the delicate forms of graptolites, etc. In Pennsylvania the formation of this limestone is 2,000 feet in thickness.

Again, the carboniferous age is principally characterized by the accumulation of vast deposits of vegetable matter which become converted into the coal of commerce. From facts like these we gain testimony that can not be questioned, that all the solid structures of the earth have been slowly built up under the play of the same radiant forms of energy that now characterize the radiant belt of mechanically working forces, so that the question remains unanswered respecting the whence of these vast deposits of matter. Radiant matter and animal and vegetable life have played an important part as builders, but from whence come the *materials* with which they build? Nebulous matter here cuts no figure, star-dust and cometary matter give no evidence now of furnishing material for the building up of any forms of life. The vast supplies of carbon of the carboniferous age, and, indeed, for the building of the vegetable and animal structures of our own age, must come from some unmeasured sources either within or above this belt of earth formation. The Archæan age of the earth surely could contribute nothing from its locked up stores of matter towards building the structures of the ages above it.

If it be answered that the sun furnished these supplies from the body of the sun, we have only to reply that the law of gravity teaches that such building has been done by attraction and atomic affinities, and by the same agencies must matter be built up on the body of the sun, and the distinctive individuality of the two bodies forbids the assumption even, of such a transference of matter.

The answer then is, and the only possible answer, that, from the same currents of radiant matter that reveal energy by resistance, affording light and heat, come also the elementary atoms of all forms of matter. We have endeavored to magnify the thought that back of all aggregative matter and through all space there is a system of attracting and repelling currents that constitute all mechanical power, and even all sensible displays of power. If we read our illustrations of mechanical power upward from that of the water wheel to the steam engine and finally to the electro-dynamic generator of electrical currents, we find that the energy back of each couple of power is an invisible agency of the radiant matter of attraction and repulsion. It is repulsion in the lifting work of the sunbeam; it is attraction in the flowing currents of the river. It is repulsion in the frictional cylinder transferred from the power of the water wheel to the power of the heated water in the boiler of the engine. It is attraction in the magnets of the electrical generator that is broken by the stronger power of repulsion of the engine. It is attraction that leads the electrical currents through the conducting wires; it is repulsion revealed by the resistance of the carbon burner of the electric lamp in the electric light. In this entire series of counter working forces we can but discover the presence of a world of power, constant, exhaustless and eternal in the environment of all forms of matter. Question this entire problem of the forces of matter as we may, but one answer is given respecting the whence of material energy and that answer is, that it is from the vast sea of radiant energy surrounding bodies of matter in space.

Now, if we can establish the relation between matter and energy in space that exists between matter and energy under the ponderable forms of matter, then we can gain conceptions of radiant matter filling all of space, co-existent and co-eternal therewith.

With our old ideas of space as a vacuum and of matter as a chance product of chaos and all of creative energy as held in reserve or directed according to the decisions of a divine mind, and held to creative work under the guidance of a divine will, it is necessary that we make haste slowly in furnishing proof that primal forces and primal forms of matter co-exist in space, endowing it with a materiality as real and as complete in their lines of motion and methods of systematic order, as that of the great globes of matter that scientists have studied as presenting the entire problem of creation.

The conception, for some cause, has been gained that force or energy is possible, separate from matter; hence the imponderable forces, such as light, heat, electricity, magnetism, chemical affinity and life are regarded as nonmaterial, having no representative form in matter, and consequently exercise their sovereignty outside of, and independent of material conditions.

By means of such conception we have had but half of the problem of creation set before us and consequently no satisfactory solution could be obtained.

Physicists have studied the laws of matter under the sensible forms of matter as they have come into place under the commanding presence of the great law of attraction; they have also observed their combustion under the working presence of the great law of repulsion, and have seen them transformed into a condition of glowing radiance, and at this point they have lost the conception of a preserved materiality.

They find an energy in matter revealing its presence under the two forms of attraction and repulsion; from either form mechanical power may be secured of vast importance in promoting the industries of civil life. In the belt of the mechanical forces these two forms of power balance each other, and under their working presence the conditions of matter conform to the form of energy doing work. Below this working belt the one commanding energy of attraction predominates and matter is held under the latent energy of attraction in stable forms; above this belt of the working forces the energy of repulsion predominates and matter must either be annihilated or take on the peculiar forms of radiant matter under the energy of repulsion.

Again, it appears that within this working belt of the mechanical forms of force, that all power results from disturbance of the natural working conditions of material energy. We condition the displays of force by interposing resistants to the performance of normal work. By this means we divert power, or draw it off from the great flowing currents of universal energy. The grand energy of attraction of universal gravitation drives the water wheel, while the grand energy of atomic repulsion that is revealed in the radiance of the sunbeam, drives our steam engines.

In the earth there is stored up, as in a vast reservoir, the power of attraction. The measure of this power is, according to the mathematical statement of the law of universal gravitation, simply the measure of the earth's mass. The power of attraction stored up in the sun and all the planetary bodies, including satellites, of the solar system, is as the measure of the mass of their several bodies.

"Directly as mass and inversely as the squares of distance from their several centers," these bodies act upon each other in the great social system of sun and planets.

Now, as the sun in mass far exceeds all of the planetary bodies in the aggregate of their measure, it follows that the planets working under this power of attraction alone, instead of taking up orbital paths of motion around the sun, would be drawn on radial lines towards the sun's center. Hence, we here call attention to the fact that all forms of matter taking up paths of motion in straight lines are moved under the power of attraction, while those moving on orbital lines move under the joint action of attraction and repulsion. With two bodies of matter of unequal size in a field of mutual attraction and at the same time hypothetically at rest, an initial impulse of motion equal to the power of attraction of the smaller body being imparted to it, would necessarily take up a curvilinear motion except the impulse was directly toward the center of the larger body or in direct opposition to such center. The path of a cannon ball upon the surface of the earth discharged on different lines of elevation, will be similar to the path of such a body of matter set in motion in free space, on like lines of impulse.

Again, if such impulse is imparted to the so-called inertia of the body, in a line of impulse above the line of a tangent to a circle or at an obtuse angle to the radial line joining the center of the two bodies, the attraction of the larger body would act as a constant retardation of motion, and consequently a constantly increased deflection of motion from the line of impulse towards the larger body, while each point of deflection gained would be increased by the hypothetical inertia of the body until the line of motion would become the radial line of attraction towards the center of the larger body.

CHAPTER XX.

FORM AND MOTION OF PLANETS DETERMINE THEIR ORIGIN.

BUT our problem teaches that one-half of the power causing the earth's motion around the sun is the power of attraction, a power that is inherent in matter. Again, it teaches that the hypothetical primary impulse imparted to the earth's mass at creation upon the line of a tangent to its orbit is at once changed to a broken line of motion, and by the material energy of attraction is constrained to act at every point of impulse at right angles to a radial line joining the center of the earth with the center of the sun.

But not only does the straight line of primary impulse become broken by material energy, but the hypothetical inertia of matter, or its "property of passiveness," is at once advanced to the dignity of a repellent energy of equal strength to the universal energy of attraction of gravitation while, *The sweep of the great circular paths of the planets around the sun reveal a constant energy of repulsion equal to the sun's energy of attraction.*

These two forces of material energy deny the passivity of matter, and proclaim the law of inertia as taught by our scientists, a myth. There are from some whence lines of orbital energy urging the planets along their circular paths of motion in space equal to the radial lines of attracting energy between sun and planets. As we find attraction and repulsion upon the earth equal forces, both in the laboratory of the scientist and in the power machines of the mechanic, so we assume that the machinery of the solar system works out its grand results, subject to the harmonious co-working energy of these two universal forces of magnetic attraction and electrical repulsion.

Now we find no difficulty in conceiving of all the planetary bodies of space as yielding perfect and unchanging obedience to occult forces. These forces establish for the solar system a great equatorial plane of rest in which the centers of the planets describe their orbital line of motion around the sun; they also fix the poles of axial motion of all the planets at right angles to such equatorial plane. Again, we can conceive of these occult forces working through all of matter that is gathered in planetary form, and even saturating such planetary bodies with occult energy as the steel of the magnet is saturated with such forces. Once more we can conceive of these occult forces weaving a network of force currents between planetary bodies, separated from each other by millions of miles. In fact we recognize the radiant presence of such forces in the pathway of each rising and setting sun, and hence we ask, may we not conceive of all of space traversed with great floods of radiant matter flowing with immense power in systematic order and under as perfect guidance as the streams of water or the currents of the wind upon the face of the earth? We have already seen that the radiant matter revealed in the sunbeam is the source of all power upon the earth, and we know that the radiant lines of the electrical current carry with them a power that no ingenuity of man can measure; and if we allow thought to take in the declaration of Revelation that "In the beginning God created the heavens and the earth," we can only conceive of the work of creation wrought out by the agency of occult lines of radiant matter touched by the intellectual impulse of an infinite will power. It becomes necessary that we should endeavor to fix lines of thought in our minds respecting matter in space, because, we have been accustomed to limit our conceptions of matter to the testimony of the senses, and hence have been perplexed with the problem of world creation out of nothing, and of the guiding the planets in their orbits by the force of attraction between bodies of matter on the one hand, and passivity of matter and original divine impulse on the other. How universal attraction of gravitation could find a balance in universal passivity of matter, and how divine impulse could impart orbital velocity to planetary bodies by a spiritual agency, equal to the attraction of gravitation between bod ies of matter, giving them a compound energy of half spirit and half matter, securing a velocity of thirty miles in a second of time, we have found no teacher of science ready to tell us; and still this class of teaching satisfies many minds and will restrain such minds from attempting to follow the simple lines of thought that our subject reveals. If we pause here and gather up the lines of thought that we have let drop here and there in our nec-. essarily broken and irregular steps of progress toward an intellectual acquaintance with the unseen primary forces and forms of matter in its radiant state, we may note

1. That all imponderable forms of matter take on the form of currents in free space.

2. That these currents move with immense velocity constituting great floods of power always flowing towards attracting centers of matter on radial lines, or around such centers on orbital lines, so long as such lines of motion are unbroken, or the normal state of the forces in relation to each other, remains undisturbed.

3. That the great floods that obey gravital attractions and flow upon radial lines constituting universal attraction of gravitation are laden with virgin elements of matter that are poured in constant floods upon the surfaces of all bodies of matter and through the circulatory currents that build such bodies into varied organic structures. These floods are the floods of energy and material lines of force revealed in the magnet and that cause all forms of matter to preserve a sensitive union to universal energy and universal primary conditions of matter that constitute the first things of creation.

4. The great floods of virgin matter and energy that flow in orbital currents around the sun and planetary bodies, and at right angles to the radial floods above noticed, are floods of electrical power that constitute the repellent force of matter in space that balances the stored up attractions of matter in planetaty forms, and that give velocity and guidance to the planets in their orbits around the sun. *The sun and planets are vast magnets revolving in a sea of electro-magnetic forces.* The lines of force that constitute the power of the magnet, reveal their organic unity and completeness in a constantly preserved

balance between axial *magnetic* currents of energy and orbital *electrical* currents of energy.

The currents of electricity and magnetism always reveal in their working harmony both duality and unity. They are as inseparable from each other as positive and negative currents of electricity are, or as attraction and repulsion are from the force currents of the magnet, and yet they perform their work by paths of motion crossing each other at right angles as the radial lines and the latitudinal lines of planetary bodies intersect at every conceivable point of contact.

This proposition, that needs no proof, marks a clear and well defined distinction between electricity and magnetism, that exists between them as equal material sovereignties united in the one universal sovereignty of force that presides over matter in all of its creative changes and sublime velocities. Under the joint sovereignty of these two correlate forces of matter, magnetism maintains the sovereignty of attraction over matter in body, while electricity maintains the sovereignty of repulsion over matter in space. The lines of magnetic strength work on the radial lines of attraction while the lines of electrical energy work upon orbital lines of repulsion.

This gives us two equal material sovereignties of universal power, joining together the two kingdoms of the heavens and the earth—of matter in body and matter in space, in an intersphering unity of harmoniously working forces that can suffer no disturbance equal to the dust of the balance.

The ultimates of thought here reached are, atomic or

molecular individuality working together giving organic unity and universal harmony.

The interchanging local disturbances between attraction and repulsion in the changing states of matter upon the surfaces of planetary bodies produce no disturbance of the sovereign balance of forces; indeed it is the co-working of these forces that reveals to us all of our knowledge of creative work. Under these forces we acquaint ourselves with the atom and the world of atoms, alike marvels of obedience to one grand sovereignty of order in the evolution of all forms of being and all orders of worlds.

With these conceptions of electrical and magnetic working lines of energy as they are revealed in the magnet we have only to think of the sun and planets held in charge of these two correlate forces to give to our minds clear conceptions of the behavior of radiant matter in space.

The sun and planets are vast magnets because they are held in charge of electro-magnetic forces. The forces are not from these bodies but these bodies are from the forces. The primary state of matter is the radiant state, and the building of matter into body is under the working lines of order that these forces take on when in charge of matter under organic affinities. Magnetic lines of force fix centers and build around such centers, drawing matter on lines of radial energy equally from surrounding radiant matter in space, consequently they take on globular form and become growing worlds, deriving their aggregating power and increase of form from the radiant sea of matter in which they are fixed in their axial and orbital lines of motion by electro-magnetic forces constituting them working electro-magnets. As solid matter takes on form so does radiant matter take on normal lines of motion around it, as around an electro-magnet so that as each magnet has a field of magnetic influence so does each planetary body establish its magnetic field of working forces. And such magnetic field conforms to the law of attraction of gravitation, *viz.*, directly as mass and inversely as the squares of distance.

We desire to extend thought into and across the field of sensible measures that are mapped out by the material force currents of sun and planets as vast magnets. It is the firm conviction of my own mind that the sun's field of gravital influence is as truly matter as his solid organic structure, and that such matter is in ceaseless activity, flowing in currents of sovereign energy and in exact lines of order and harmony, constituting the creating, governing, changing and revolving forces that appear in the more tangible forms of matter. Without the sensible presence of these floods of radiant lines of matter that come to us in the light of the sun, that flow in currents of strength through our bodies as they keep in play the inflowing and outflowing floods of atomic elements of matter that are laden with incoming supplies of daily life, and the outgoing wastes attendant upon Nature's methods of work, our bodily forms would be wholly unfit for the dwelling place of our spirits. Our hearing, seeing, tasting, smelling, feeling that connect us with the world of matter are entirely dependent upon this radiant form of matter that constitutes the social tie that pervades all forms of life and all ranks and orders of Nature's complete work.

The solar system is no exception to the social system of family ties that is characteristic of creative work in the various ranks of life upon the earth.

The sun and planets constitute a family of worlds bound together by mutual lines of sensitive intercourse and dependent relationship. So sensitive is this relation between the sun and the earth, that the magnetic needle notes the progress of the sun in his daily circuit from rising to setting, by a constant daily variation through an angle of ten or fifteen minutes, moving in one direction during the early part of the day, and back again during the latter part of the day with the motion reversed in the southern hemisphere.

This variation of the needle must arise from the variation of the magnetic currents of the earth, influenced by the changing magnetic currents of the sun.

The term "magnetic field" was devised by Faraday and is defined as any space at every point of which exists a fine magnetic force, while a line of magnetic force is a line drawn through a magnetic field in the direction of the force at each point through which it passes.

Before the time of Faraday natural philosophers were satisfied with the mere statement that magnets acted at a distance, and followed generally the same law as ruled in the action of gravitation throughout the celestial spaces, that is to say, that the intensity of the magnetic action decreased inversely as the squares of the distance from the center of the magnet; but Faraday, "in his mind's eye," says Prof. Maxwell, "saw lines of force traversing all space where the mathematicians saw centers of force attracting at a distance; Faraday saw a medium when they saw nothing but distance; Faraday sought the seat of the phenomena in real actions going on in the medium, they were satisfied that they had found it in a power of action at a distance impressed on the electric fluids." We may here add that Faraday was a student of radiant forces, while the mathematicians only conceived of quantitive measures.

The foregoing reference to the conceptions of Faraday by Alfred M. Mayer in the Scientific American of October 4, 1879, will aid us in gaining a correct conception of the systematic order that radiant matter takes on in its masterly guidance of the planetary systems of worlds in space. "All material phenomena come into our field of vision as effects produced by an unseen potency. This potency has taken on material form in the mind of Faraday and consists of a universal presence surrounding bodies of matter in space weaving around them lines of force of infinite fineness, equal to the measure of the elementary atoms of which such bodies have been formed." Thus it is no mystery that the magnetic field of linear forces induced by the magnetic strength of atoms in body should be adequate to the complete upholding and guidance of any body in space, no matter how great may be its magnitude; while this gives us an enlarged vision of the matter actually bound to the gravital center of every planetary body; for we must regard the magnetic field of radiant matter surrounding the body as truly a part of its complete structure as are the solids, liquids and gases of its sensible form.

Again, we cannot complete our vision of radiant matter surrounding each planetary body, unless we observe carefully the self-determining order assumed by the two grand correlating floods of radiant lines that fix axial position and give orbital motion alike to all bodies of matter in space. Magnetic attraction drawing upon radial lines, along which the rays of light pass from body to body and which unite the bodies of the solar system in one vast magnetic field, is complemented by electrical repulsion, that, as we have already noticed, attracts the planets in their orbital paths across such radial lines with a strength equal to the strength of magnetic or gravital attraction stored up in the solid nucleus of the planetary body. The system of electrical and magnetic currents of the electro-magnet reveals the systematic order with which these currents preside over all organic unions of elements into sensible forms, and by which all working forces in Nature secure their unfailing power. The power of the magnetic lines of the floods of light passing between the earth and sun coupled with the cross floods of electrical currents that establish orbital paths of planetary revolution, and of the destructive cyclone that sweeps along over the earth, uprooting trees and lifting the staunchest structures from their foundations, alike disclose the same combination of force-currents that give strength to the magnet. The source of this elementary power is as unfailing as space is immeasurable.

That we have done but little more than attempt to lead scientific thought over a field already existing, though in a shadowy form in scientific minds, we add an extract from Prof. Tyndall. Referring to the force currents of the magnet he says, "The aspect of these curves so fascinated Faraday that the greater portion of his intellectual life was devoted to pondering over them. He invested the space through which they run with a kind of materiality, and the probability is, that the progress of science by connecting the phenomena of magnetism with the luminiferous ether will prove these 'lines of force,' as Faraday loved to call the magnetic curves to represent a condition of this substratum of all radiant action.''

"The condition of the substratum of all radiant action" is positively fixed in the metallic lines of magnetic phenomena, so the substratum of all organisms of matter whether of a revolving world or a grain of mustard seed is fixed by the same metallic lines of energy. The solid form of the magnet and the radiant form of its field of forces are alike parts of a single unity of organic power. It is in fact in the organism of the radiant portion of the magnet that its power resides.

The radiant field of the magnet is translated into the power of the magnet, as the sun's field of light is translated upon the earth into the mechanical forces that are resultants of sun energy. It is therefore scarcely possible to evade the conviction of the materiality of all forms of radiant energy. The entire line of our work leads us to the recognition of the presence of matter with all forms of material force. As the material world could not be created out of nothing, so material force can not display its power within or across an utter void. A force without matter is as unthinkable as the evolution of matter from a perfect vacuity. We can not think of a subjective without an objective, neither can we think of force acting where there is no object to translate the force.

CHAPTER XXI.

LIFE AND RADIANT MATTER.

THE position that light occupies in the process of evolutionary or creative work is central and primary. The story of Moses respecting the creation teaches that light was the first agency called into place by the creator. Science also teaches that the sun through the agency of light and heat is the source of all power and the cause of all forms of life upon the earth.

We have endeavored to magnify the thought that radiant energy and radiant matter are inseparable from each other, we even go a step further and affirm that radiant matter and energy were primal to all of matter in organic forms. Immortal matter and energy as revealed in the lines of light are the "something" out of which and by which the worlds have been built, and the same lines of light continue to carry forward their immortal work in the unfolding of life and form, that are to us the conditions of the grand problem of creation. The radiance of the light is simply a condition of radiant matter reporting its working presence to our senses. It is a vibration, an impulse that touches the organs of sense and passes with the velocity of thought. By this passing radiance we gain a glimpse of the lines of force that are carrying forward the constant work of creation, or of generation and reproduction which are synonymous with creation. Under the hand of the experimenter a ray of light gives light, heat and chemical affinity. It also obeys the laws of matter, suffering attraction, repulsion, absorption, reflection, etc., and while obeying the laws of matter it envelopes all forms of matter with its radiance and its lines of energy afford the social tie that binds all forms of matter and all conditions of life into a unity of being. It also gives identity of being and preserves such identity in the midst of the widest diversity. Each animal, plant, or germ of life receives its needed supply of energy and atoms from the light to be enfolded into its evolving life form in exact measures, no more and no less than the being or object craves.

These all wait upon the light and receive their sustenance in due season. The statement of the law of gravitation will apply to the distribution of the elements of light. Each object attracts and is attracted by every other object within its field of influence, or within its magnetic field. It is claimed by some of our best scientists that light has both a forward and a backward motion. We would translate this seeming motion of light into that of magnetic impulse and regard each form of matter possessed by a polarizing energy and consequently constantly wrought upon by polarizing currents. These currents in the living forms of matter establish the magnetic centers of the living organisms, and these become life centers and all of the circulatory flow of fluids that nourish and stimulate the varied functions of life in the living body are kept in constant play by the self working power of electro-magnetic currents.

The machinery of the living organism of matter is no exception to machinery prepared by human hands, in requiring a power constantly applied to produce constant work.

The pitcher at the fountain and the wheel at the cistern derive their command over life from the self-adjusting power of attraction and repulsion that waits upon every polarized form of matter. The pulsating currents of the hair-like stings of the nettle that Prof. Huxley has seized upon as an interpreter of microscopic life, as truly as the circulation of the blood in the animal economy, derive their power from this one universal form and source of power. Protoplasm derives its power to take on new formations and multiply its elementary organism into the more complex from this dual power of polarization. I am aware of the fact that many scientific minds have decided against the claims we here make for this "material basis of life" but we make our statements, leaving them with the inquiry, if not these, what?

CHAPTER XXII.

EVOLUTION OF LIFE.

ANOTHER condition of the problem is, atoms of matter conditioning sovereign material energy ; for diversity of atoms that are elementary to diversities of substances must have inhered in the atoms and not in the supreme harmonic energy. In crystallization the atoms always determine the crystalline forms, with mathematical accuracy.

Again, the above conditions give the thought of space as illimitable, matter as immeasureable and imponderable, and material energy as compassing all with its unifying sovereignty of power, endowed from each atom with an individuality of unit strength, thus constituting it a factor in the great problem of universal creative work. The atoms, as factors, recognize the necessity of their unification into the elementary substances of the chemist that have been detected and numbered as the sixty-four elementary substances of creation that have given phenomenal forms of matter.

The division of matter into substances gives us further the idea of attracting and repellent conditions of universal energy in both binding together and dividing the elementary substances into lines of material unity. In such binding of atoms, likes are bound to likes, and also separated from unlikes by a sovereign energy of attraction and repulsion that characterizes the behavior of elementary currents of matter in space.

The law of electrical currents, which we venture to regard as elementary currents of matter, is found by experiment to be, "That currents moving in the same direction attract, while those moving in opposite directions repel each other." Electrical currents of matter interflow, positive and negative flowing in opposite directions and exactly complementing each other. Again, atoms bound together in linear order, demand polar contacts of the atoms, as in the joining of magnet to magnet at their poles. Such joining fulfills the conditions of electric currents, in giving completed circuits, while the positive and negative currents flowing in opposite directions of equal couples of strength and velocity, obeserve their separate identity, giving the first complete equation of elementary matter and elementary energy, prior to, and separate from, the building of atoms into organic world-forms.

This elementary combination of atoms and energy gives us a clear conception of matter and material energy constituting a duality of both energy and substance counterflowing in space in perfect order and undisturbed harmony. In this combination of elements into linear order of substances, we have visualized that great deep of darkness out of which, and by which the worlds were made. The temperature and the darkness of now stellar space with all its pervading lines of electrical energy are the same as at the beginning. Even now, the work of creation goes forward under the guiding touch of electrical affinities, drawing both the strength and the substance of organic structures from radiant matter in charge of electrical currents; and again, when organic structures are consumed by oxidation or combustion, they pass again into electrical currents in space. Creation is from the dark and cold embrace of the swiftly moving currents of the great deep of space to which there must be a return of elements when there is a complete disintegration of creation's work.

This leads us to the contemplation of the second problem set before us in the changes of matter from its occult, elementary, radiant state, to its three sensible and working states, *viz.*, gaseous, liquid and solid.

The work of involution of diverse atoms from the distinct substances of linear currents into the complex unions of substances now appearing in organic forms of matter, reveals a new law of atomic control.

In space likes are bound to likes by polar contacts constituting lines or currents of matter. In all organic or molecular structures, *unlikes* are bound together by *lateral* bindings or attractions, as magnets are bound together, side by side, by reversal of poles. By this process of binding, the joining of two oppositely charged atoms produces a molecule of double magnetic strength to that of the separate atoms. This molecule of enhanced power seeks a union with another of opposite elective affinity, and another step is taken in the work of systematic aggregation. At each step in the process a new form of matter comes into place with new powers and new possibilities of creative work. It is in this order that the entire complex work of creation is carried forward under the systematic harmony of inherent affinities and exterior balancing repulsions; the former we call magnetization, the latter electrization. In pursuing this line of thought we come to the boundary line between electricity and magnetism as observed in their united sovereignty over matter. It is broken currents of electricity that give us elementary atoms as magnets, while the restoration of such atoms to currents gives us electricity. In space positive and negative currents balance all velocities by their equal and oppositely flowing lines of matter. These counter floods of energy interflow, equals in strength but diverse in substance. These constitute the elementary parental unity that everywhere appears as generative affinities in organic being and affinity. In body, magnetic affinities gather matter into new substances and establishing a new order of free currents that are held under the control of the bodies thus formed. Hence we find magnetic currents reveal their strength in all cases on radial lines leading to and from the gravital center of the organized body. Newton's discovery of the great law of attraction of gravitation, was a discovery of the law of magnetic currents in their relation to the bodies of matter that have been built up under the working energy of magnetic or elective affinities.

From the mathematical demonstration confirming this discovery we learn that bodies attract bodies directly as mass, *i. e.*, they attract in organic forms as they attracted in their dissociate atoms. There is not masked in the created form the strength of a single atom, but such strength is joined with its associate atoms in long working lines of attraction, drawing from the great dark depths of space elements of virgin matter to increase the body and enhance the strength of the organism into which they are socially bound. Electricity in space may thus be converted into magnetism in bodies, and magnetism in bodies by dissociation may be converted into electricity in space. Conservation of force and conservation of atoms in all changes of matter scientific minds have already reached by way of experiment, and we here learn that the adjusted balance between electricity and magnetism gives us the dividing line between matter and energy in body and matter and energy in space.

In body magnetic currents are the commanding unity of creative energy that hold all the working forces of both electricity and magnetism to a perfect order of grouping around fixed centers of aggregation. By just so much as the work of organic structures is carried forward under the work of magnetic affinities, by just so much is electrical atomic energy in orbital currents bound in completed circuits to sweep around such centers with a repellent and balancing energy equal to the working magnetic strength of the gravital centers around which they flow. Here is revealed a general law that is never violated or changed in the complex work of the multiplied developments of Nature's building.

The initial centers of magnetic attraction are always foundation points at which creative work begins, and the first group of atoms gathered around such centers are the foundation stones upon which all creative structures are built. Toward such centers the lines of magnetic attraction always move, laden with virgin atoms of matter as the materials of building; from such atoms selection and rejection, under the law of magnetic affinities, assorts the atoms and carries them to their place in the growing structures.

By following out this line of thought we reach the beginnings of creation and find them the beginnings of substance, and also the beginnings of material energy; and we learn that from them have come all the grand results of creation's work.

The worker and the works thus stand revealed to human thought as compassing the entire field of infinites and holding in their grasp all of the possibilities of evolving world structures and of life forms. All the radiant garments of creation in the diverse colors that now appear to human vision are woven from the same garments of immortality that wrapped themselves around the initial centers of world creations.

As worlds were created, so worlds are now carrying forward the work of their unfinished structures.

What we now call growth was at the beginning Nature's work of creation, and could we unfold the presence of the occult forces that secure the growth of a blade of grass or of the formation of the tiniest seed with its inwrapt life germ, we should be brought face to face with the same forces and the same order of work that appeared at the beginning.

The powers and the wisdom of creation are now revealed in every evolving form of life, and infinity in its broadest and fullest conception touches each growing seed as it at the beginning touched each growing world center.

We find the deepest mystery of life in the constantly revolving circle of its periodic changes of growth and decay —of life and death—of seed-beginning and seed-producing, as opposite points in the circle of life, with the growing and dying life-form intervening between these two points of rest and renewal. In this circle there is involved a duality of being or of force, without which there could be no renewal of life. The new life cannot be possible without the separate unfolding of two distinct organisms, that on reaching matureness of structure meet in generative embrace imparting a new seed-life. Now, while we cannot trace the lines of union that are mingled in this new life-germ, we are justified in affirming that radiant matter must have bridged the chasm between the old lives and the new, between the parental duality and the germinal individuality.

The same radial lines that give the parental image in the mirror by an instantaneous flash of light, give also the parental image in the germ-life that evolves a new paternity.

The blending of the positive and negative circles of the magnetic circuit, evolving energy and work where broken circuits re-unite, thus find their place in the mysterious circles of life. As we have seen that all material organisms take on their organic form around gravital centers, drawing their atoms of aggregation from electrical currents so the life germs of all living organisms take up their order of growth from the magnetic centers of their growing forms, insomuch that the organizing potency of life germs is evolved from the working potency of magnetic circuits and thus radiant matter is carried through all the circuits of life in body along the working lines of magnetic strength establishing a sensitive union to the central life germ.

Thus the field of the radiant forces is the field of the mysterious births of all parental life The life force is not paternal to life currents of organizing strength that are regarded in our line of thought as magnetic currents, but the life comes into place at the focal points where the converging oppositely moving magnetic lines touch each other under the guidance of magnetic attractions or at points where opposite polarities blend into a single constantly pulsating bodily form with its pulsing forces. It is to be kept in mind that we are here seeking acquaintance with circulatory forces that are self organizing and self guiding and at the same time are materially conditioned under their own laws of guidance. An infinite number of life forms may come into place on the life-plane of these circulatory forces, while the one great system of attracting and repelling currents of magnetization is as fixed in its lines of force and orders of work as the rocks at the foundations of the mountains. In fact, all that is strong and abiding in matter rests upon these currents of energy, so all that there is of life is dependent upon the constancy and perpetually pulsating flow of these same unseen potencies of creation.

We have already gained a glimpse of the thought that elementary atoms of matter possess a sovereign identity, insomuch that they condition universal energy.

Atoms of matter come into orgaizations of matter solely under their own inherent power of selection. Positive and negative elementary atoms are as potent in their affinities of combination as positive and negative electro-magnetic currents are in their lines of motion.

This being conceded, and surely no chemist will interpose a doubt, it follows that the growing life structures must be conditioned by the atomic elements gathered into the germinal structure. Identity of being must depend upon the elements grouped by their selective affinities in the material bodily organism. Mark the order in all propagation of species and you will find that the life-germ in its material organism always determines the order of successive individualities of the species; and, hence, the first of the line of species must have been determined by the elements of matter grouped in the infinitesimal germ as it took on life. Now we have come face to face with another unifying thought which is, that as the character of the varied species of life is consequent upon certain material groupings of matter in the germ, it follows that life in some form comes into place as a necessity, from such groupings, under the grand law of magnetization. Life is a universal unity, as light, heat, gravitation, polarization, etc., are unities. The life of the infinitesimal germ of the tiniest form of being is from the same universal force that supplies life to the grandest orders of being that are grouped upon the great life-plane. By consulting the composition of the rocks we find elementary crystalline work intimately joined to elementary life-forms, so that even the rocky foundations of the mountains have come into place above the life-plane of creation. From this lowest plane of life in rock formation the series is upward in creation, line after line in an unbroken series till the crowning work is reached in the thinking, reasoning animal that we call man. The order of ascending life-organisms is from the simple to the complex. From the lowest form of vegetable life to the highest, there is a constant succession of new forms of being, while to each ascending form there is an endowment of self-perpetuation. There is paternity and seed-fruitage that fixes the classifications of plants into sub-kingdoms, genera, and species, while they fall into groups variously related to one another as brothers, cousins, and so forth. This plant-paternity that preserves the continuance of species, involves the necessity of the transference of organism in the electro-magnetic condition of germ-life.

The plant-likeness in the germ must spring from focal sensory lines of matter proceeding from every sensory atom of the plant-form to the infinitesimal seed-germ, with the faithfulness of the lines of light that form sensory images of objects upon the retina of the eye, producing sun-pictures of perfect likeness to each object within the range of vision. The preservation of perfect unity of life and likeness between the growing plant and the germ of seed-life within the plant, amid the unnumbered varieties of plant structure can be visualized alone under the radial lines of magnetization that we regard as identical with the radiant matter of the sunlight.

To this radiant condition of matter, all living organic forms must descend to find the plane of germ-life. As the gravital centers of all planetary bodies rest in the neutral plane of the sun's equator that fixes the plane of the planetary orbits, so all of germ-life finds its beginning in the plane of radial matter where positive and negative magnetic currents blend into unity. In the vegetable kingdom the circle of life from germ to fruitage is from radiant centers of matter to radiant centers, the one an evolving center, the other an involving. The radial lines of matter converging from without the plant from space in the unfolding life, and from within the plant to the germ in the infolding life. The circles of life through the successive periods of seed and fruitage bear a close relationship to the periodic circles of time-measure fixed in the solar system by the revolution of the planets. All creative work is fixed and carried forward in constantly revolving circles. The line of progress is from the smaller to the greater. The greater circles infolding all of the smaller, and the smaller unfolding and multiplying producing the greater. In this intervolving, evolving and blending there is a constant preservation of identities of the separate orders of life and ranks of organic structure.

This identity always being preserved and commanded by the gravital or germinal life center. All classes of gravital or germinal energy are weighed or measured, in all forms of matter, from center to center, thus determining their relative values and orders of sovereignty in the grand scale of complex being.

Under this order of progressive circles and determinate centers, the harmony of creative work is preserved in the constantly progressive works of creation. Our thoughts of creation begin with the atoms of the sixty-four substances, each atom and substance having an identity of form and energy that are fixed and immortal.

From these identities of matter and energy the worlds have been fashioned. The first grand division of these atoms and substances appears in that grand parental duality that exists between positive and negative lines of matter that take on the form of electrical currents counterflowing in space. The second grand division appears when these currents are broken up into atomic forms under the influence of the energy of magnetization, and being joined in selective generative unions group themselves around gravital centers of aggregation becoming individualizing potencies.

These grand divisions of matter belong to the low plane of electrial and magnetic potencies that are native to the cold and the darkness of the great deep of unmeasured space, but when centers of aggregation are fixed and gravital attractions spring into place and revolving globes of matter divide themselves into families, while atoms of matter flow together under strong elective or chemical affinities, then as now heat is generated, light is evolved and by this means there is a progressive building toward the ultimate plane of germinal organisms. When the higher plane is reached then follow in their order, commencing with the elementary groupings of atoms into bioplastic family organisms, the entire complex orders of life forms, the dual parental potency of procreation belonging to each order of living forms. In the progress of the grand series of life's work the steps of each order of progression are rigidly consecutive, from the simplest organism to the most complex. The more complex being sustained from an assimilation of the rudimentary, or less complex forms of organic life.

It is well understood that the higher forms of animal life cannot have come into place in the scale of being save through the assimilation of the lower forms of life constituting the vegetable kingdom.

We have already gained a glimpse of the thought that the varied forms of life take on complexity of form, and perpetuate the same through germ-life, hence, it is by no means an improbable inference that the diverse orders of being upon the earth have taken on their peculiarity of organism from the nature of the organic forms taken into their being from their food-supplies. The modification of plant-food is secured in plant-forms of life, so as to prepare it for the support of animal life. Without such modification of the elements of matter, by converting them into organic forms of life, the complex animal organisms could not be built. The plant feeds on carbon, silex, hydrogen, oxygen, etc. These are taken up from earth and sun by the plant, through leaf and rootlet, and pass into the delicate life currents that flow through the living structure, adding cell to cell, perfecting bud and twig, leaf and flower, weaving the entire life of the plant from the joint elementary currents of sun and earth, from seed-germination to seed-fruitage; but the elements thus built into forms of plant life, representing a completed circle of life, while also necessary to animal life, and constituting animal food could not be taken up into the animal organism without first passing through the creative potency of germ-life in rearing vegetable structures out of such food elements as earth and sun can jointly give in elementary forms that are without life—the same elements out of which the rocks and minerals are built. Thus the seemingly impassable gulf between the lifeless kingdom of the rocks, earths and minerals, and the complex animal kingdom, is bridged over by the germinal forces that have come into place on the low plane of vegetable life, and these from the still lower plane of rock formations.

The food supplies of the vegetable kingdom only give simple organic forms of life. These forms are directly, by generation, children of the sun and earth, and all they have of life and sensory existence springs from the joint embrace and perpetual care and nurture of the procreative potencies of the oppositely charged magnetic currents of sun and earth. The germinal life and the food supply of the plant fix the boundaries of its being. There can be no evolution of plant-life into animal life. It is not scientific to search for such an order of development. The rocks and earths in their peculiar organic forms do not become plant or tree, neither do the plant and tree in their organic life structures become animals even of the lowest type. The protoplasmic elements of plant-life or plant-food are derived directly from earth and sun. These elements pass into the plant as magnetic currents through root and leaf, and in the growing structure become the elements of plant growth constituting such combinations of carbon, oxygen, nitrogen and hydrogen in elementary living forms of matter called protoplasm, as are needed to perfect the plant structures and complete the circle of plant-life.

It is important here to mark the fact that the tree or plant has no independent existence separate from sun and earth-paternity, save that which is wrapped up, latent, in the seed-germ.

Cut off the sun-currents from the leaves of the tree or the earth-currents from the rootlets, and the life of the tree is at once weakened and soon destroyed. The flow of the sap through the cells of the plant demands the working presence of elements and potencies that elude the touch of scientific experiment, proclaiming their occult presence alone to the inner eye of reason in the mind of the experimenter.

Within the plant, shut in by delicate cell-walls of fine membranous texture, the food of the plant is carried in constantly flowing and counterflowing rivulets. From these flowing currents the work of plant assimilation goes systematically forward, building up the plant-structure from the germinal seed center, both upward toward the sun and downward toward the center of the earth, observing a constant balance between the upward and downward growths of the unfolding organism. These rivulets are kept in flow by a sensitive guidance of a centralized energy within the plant that takes its definitive guiding lines of work from the germinal life-center of the plant; hence, the building of the cell walls and the flow of the plant-food are contemporaneous in their appearance to the eye of the scientist that observes the progressive work of plant-structure, as the plant grows by adding cell to cell, each cell seeming to possess within itself the power of self-propagation. This power of self-propagation reveals an order of life that bridges the gulf between the living plant-organism and the elementary atoms of matter that are built into plant structures. This order of life seems to include both environing cell and the environed circulating sap of the plant, insomuch that they build within each other and from each other as if they were the material work of some spiritual builder.

This brings us to the border-land of creative work, and it is here that true science brings all human thought in its inquiry after the true basis of life. The problem of life in the protoplasm that constitutes the food of all living organisms, when solved, will unify human thought and break down partition walls between innumerable schools of thought that are now dividing society into warring factions. Spirit and matter, though they may represent two entities in creation, surely work together in full accord in the fashioning of all material structures.

The protoplasmic state of matter occupies so large a space in scientific investigation that it is unnecessary to say more respecting it than to note the fact that in protoplasm there are grouped elements of matter, *viz.*, oxygen, nitrogen, hydrogen and carbon, out of which living structures are reared. These constitute the elements that await the pulsating currents of life to carry them to their place in the growing forms of life. By pressing thought a step further it must be evident that protoplasm gives the material conditions of life and that without these conditions there could be no food supplies for a single growing form of life. Again, we find that life is not only dependent on food supplies of matter but upon such supplies raised to radiant conditions to secure its assimilation into living, organic forms. Life, therefore, like light, seeks a radiant plane of matter where it alone can reveal its working presence. Upon such plane all forms of life come into place as births from a common parentage, and yet each form is endowed with a personality of being peculiar to itself and with powers of reproduction that constitute them factors upon the radiant plane of creative potencies.

But it has been already indicated that there is an indwelling pulsating energy in matter in its cohesive affinities that secures organic aggregation or growth below the radiant plane of light and life. The night and the darkness constitute a part of the successive days of creative work. These precede in their order of work all the higher orders of being.

The magnet teaches that radiant matter is possessed of a constant energy of work that is normal to the cold and the darkness, and more than this that all forms of matter and all conditions of space are held in charge of matter in its radiant lines of energy. In this condition of radiant matter we find the conditioning cause of germ life in protoplasmic conditions of matter.

From this dark plane of magnetization germ centers derive their strength in pulsating currents of elementary atoms that infold individuality of germ organism and unfold living forms of being. Hence, we affirm that in this radiant elementary plane of matter to which all forms of matter are transparent as the atmosphere is to sunlight, we are to fix the material basis of all of life. Without this the problem of life finds no scientific solution, and with it the mysteries of the origin of life are no greater than its continuance.

It is unnecessary to follow the leadings of scientific thought further in this border land of elementary life and being than to fix the natural boundaries at which complex forms of organic life take up the initial lines of their progressive orders of being.

It would give us great pleasure to be able to discover the presence of indwelling intelligence at these sources of life, and we by no means deny such a presence, but such unfoldings of life from protoplasmic conditions of matter are no higher displays of a divine presence than is the continuance of life at the high plane of germinal reproduction. The low condition of life that appears in protoplasm discloses no seed of plant or egg of animal, but the atoms of matter thus grouped pass by affinities into seed structure as naturally as they pass to the unfolding life organism proceeding from seed organisms.

CHAPTER XXIII.

TESTIMONY OF THE SPECTRUM.

IN the commencement of our investigation of electrical phenomena, we had no adequate conception of the ultimates in matter and in material force to which they would lead us.

Our first conception of electrical energy compassing space with its diversely moving currents, with a correlate magnetic energy, holding all matter within the firm grasp of its attractions, and these dual manifestations of one grand commanding energy presiding over all material phenomena; we did not think of this moving, all-pervading energy as holding within its grand attractions and repulsions, the ultimates of material analysis—the primaries of all that we call matter; but in following the guidance of the working forces in matter and tracing them to their source in electrical and magnetic energy, we also found in this energy the elastic elements of all material organisms.

We at first regarded it visionary to allow such thoughts a place in our conceptions of matter, and for a time were only disposed to hint at the possibility of such an origin to matter.

The strength, elasticity and vibratory ring of the electrical cords that fill space and move through all body, led us to the conclusion that out of these must have come forth the subtle elements that electrical attractions have woven into the foundations, and have built into the rising structures of creation. We knew that all matter revealed a sympathy for the dual force of the magnet and the electrical current, so that it comes together in its unions as currents and magnets come together, positive seeking negative and negative positive, but it did not occur to us that electrical affinities in matter proclaimed an electrical origin. Even the building of the sunlight into the growing organisms of life, and treasuring itself up in the wood and the coal of past ages for the uses of man in succeeding ages, was regarded by us as simply one of the many methods of earth building, and as an evidence of providential provision for the wants of man.

But when the phenomena of light and heat became in our mind electrical phenomena, and its electro-magnetic origin was fully accepted, and its dynamic energy traced to its potential in body, the final step became a logical necessity, and the ultimates of matter were reached in the metallic strength of primary electrical forces.

The line of argument seems to us logical, and we must now verify our reasoning by comparing it with the stern logic of Nature's grand argument, as disclosed in creative work.

It must be admitted that this final step has long been a felt necessity, while it has been restrained, under the religious conviction of its trenching on holy ground. Our idea of creation as a divine work beginning in miraculous divine agency has seemed to say to us, "all scientific investigation must be satisfied with *material* second causes, resting in a Divine First Cause."

Hence, our scientists have been struggling with the second causes of fire and the gases as the first things of creation. The result is seen in the hypothesis of creation commencing with fire and ending in the burned out cinders of an exhausted conflagration. So our planetary systems have been lighted by molten suns with gaseous envelopes, and radiating energy that must sooner or later end in utter exhaustion, and the problem of their unabating energy has staggered the best minds in scientific work and imagination has come to their aid where reason could not go. The sun light, with its omnipotent building energy, has been regarded as a secondary cause rather than a primary, and depending upon the great body of the sun for its energy, instead of having been the sun builder, commissioned for its work by a self moving power fulfilling the purposes of a divine guidance. The step we have taken is from secondary material causes to a first cause.

It leads us from matter at rest, in its potential state to matter in motion in its dynamic condition. It leads us to affirm as we have already done, that the primary condition of matter is motion and motion in the unending circles of electrical potencies. We regard the divine order of building as from the dynamic to the potential.

This step lays upon us the burden of showing that the primary atoms of matter have their home in the electromagnetic forces and are evolved from them into the material organisms of creation. We cheerfully commit our hypothesis to the logic of proof, and we affirm,

1. That the dynamic energy of electricity and magnetism proclaims them possessed of a material base.

It must be granted when we come under the command of electrical law that attraction and repulsion are equally balanced forces, hence all material attractions have their balance in some way in equal material repulsions, therefore the potential attractions of all matter in body must have corresponding material repulsions in space surrounding body; and more than this, the dynamic of space must command all the potential of body, for all aggregations of matter are at the command of the dynamic energy of space and move in circuits fixed by its power.

The power of the dynamic forces is made subservient to the will of man and is found adequate to any work. The great work of engineering performed at Hellgate, near New York, is an illustration of great value. The work of months was given to preparing chambers in the solid rock under the waters of the sound where the dynamic energy could be securely placed so as to exert its energy upon the incumbent rocks. To every charge of the slumbering giant there was attached a wire as a conveyer of the electric spark at its appointed time. These wires had their leading wires carefully arranged and passed through a well protected conducting tube to a safe distance on shore to the temporary structure that the engineer had prepared for bringing them under his immediate presence and command. His battery for awakening electrical energy was prepared and awaited the opportune moment for doing its work, and when it arrived an infant's hand pressed the key of command and, with the flash of the electric spark, the earth quivered and the solid rocks with their incumbent waters were lifted in air like the playthings of a child. This is evidence that the strongest foundations of matter hold an attractive energy inferior to the repelling agency of matter that may be brought against it. While it shows that great attractive energy slumbers in matter, it also shows that the awakened energies of repulsion are equal to their mastery. The elastic strength of the treasured up dynamite is an affirmation of the treasured strength that is in matter under all of its myriad forms. In the Hellgate explosion it is matter at rest struggling against matter in motion, and struggling in vain. This leads us to inquire after the evidence of matter in the passing electrical currents of space.

I find in the Encyclopedia Britannica a statement of the researches of M. Fusiniere, who has made the study of the deposition of material substances in the passage of electrical discharges through body one of great interest and profit. We learn from him that, "Lightning contains like the common electric spark, matter in a state of extreme division and in a state of ignition and combustion.

"In the matter deposited by lightning on houses and on trees which have been struck by it" he has found "iron, sulphur and carbon. Lightning divides and subdivides itself indefinitely into sparks which end in being not much larger than those of ordinary machines and each of these sparks contains ponderable substances in the state of extreme division already mentioned."

The lightning deposits the substances with which it is charged while it passes through them and while it breaks hard bodies, and it deposits them on the surface by which it enters the body, as well as on that by which it escapes, and also on the surface of fracture.

When the resistance to its passage is not great it leaves no perceptible deposit and the quantity of matter deposited increases and is proportional to the difficulty with which the lightning traverses the body. At the same time that lightning deposits the matter which it contains it takes up new matter from the combustible bodies through which it passes, such as iron, charcoal, etc. The deposited matter tends always to expend itself in thin fibres on the surface which receives it, and it does this most readily on surfaces that are smooth and free from all asperities.

In a pear tree which had been struck by lightning in 1827, M. Fusiniere discovered very remarkable effects. Though its trunk, three feet in diameter, was torn into four parts throughout its whole length, no foreign matter nor odor could be perceived either in its roots or in the earth.

At the place where the branches joined the trunk the *substance* of the pear tree was altered to the depth of several lines. It had acquired an acid taste and a reddish color. It exhaled while burning a penetrating and peculiar odor, and it continued to burn *without flame* till it was completely consumed. The matter of the lightning had penetrated the tissue of the wood and there presented traces of iron. These and many other facts seem to prove that iron exists in space; and it is well known that the same metal, mixed with magnesia, nitrous salts and organic substances is found in rain water. Vol. 8 page 584.

The composition of meteoric substances evidently gathered in space reveals the presence of matter in the forces from which they have been ejected. Such bodies have come to the earth of many tons weight, and they only reveal the methods by which the heavenly bodies have been formed amid the rapidly moving electrical circles of space. The planetary bodies that are now sweeping space with their great orbital attractions, do not allow of the successful aggregation of any rival bodies as they, like great monopolists, gather all lesser bodies to themselves. The efforts made by our scientists to magnify these chance visitants from space into bodies of any importance in the solar system, are, in our view, wholly unwarranted by any tangible data, especially within the circle of the asteroids.

The remarkable velocity of the orbital electrical currents that move near to the sun utterly forbids the gathering and descent of any meteoric bodies of importance upon his surface. The entire space is under the tremendous working power of the sun and his inferior planets and the electrical energy of the entire field of forces contributes *directly* to their upbuilding.

The sun needs no fuel to feed his fires, save such as goes directly to feed his electro-magnetic illumimation, and this comes to him freely bearing all the primal energy that has made him the commander of a system of forces bearing triumphantly in their currents a family of worlds. Give to electricity the command of the dynamic energies of space, and to magnetism the creating, fashioning power in planetary bodies, and their illuminated surfaces the communing fields of these forces, where they meet and work together to build worlds, and meteoric showers and cometary bodies will sink into insignificance as the mere dust of the balance.

This view of the solar system gives to us great globes of matter under the control of magnetic currents and the outlying fields of space, under the control of the electrical currents, laden with the material elements of world-building, and still carrying forward the grand works of creation towards a higher and more perfect degree of order. This gives us matter in motion correlating matter at rest, and matter in these two forms expending its working energy under the joint illumination of electricity and magnetism.

This leads

2. To the work of considering spectrum analysis as giving testimony to the material nature of electrical currents. It will be granted by the candid mind, without doubt, that if the elements of matter are found in the dynamic forces that the source of material organization is in these forces.

Scientific experiment has been successfully working out the problem and all we have to do is to mark its triumphant demonstration.

The spectroscope reveals just what the chemist in his laboratory could have prophesied if he had given to electricity and light their commanding potencies in material organizations. When the galvanic battery was placed in the hands of the chemist it gave him a key with which he could unlock Nature's secrets that he had not before possessed. The very force with which Nature had built was placed in his hands as an agency to pull down that she had built. The retort and the crucible were of but little value after this in reaching the higher tests of material strength. He could evolve a more intense heat and a brighter flame from the electrodes of his battery than he had before secured under his compound blow pipes. Such a result was a complete triumph over the locked up secrets of Nature, her fortresses must all give way under such an agency in the hands of man and henceforth the wisdom and strength of the builder would reveal the very foundation stones of the structure built. The sovereignty of electricity over the forces of Nature was thus securely established under the hand of the chemist in his laboratory, but has awaited proclamation for a century. The spectroscope is well calculated to make such proclamation in the dark bands of the solar spectrum, by which the chemistry of sun, planets and stars has been revealed. It is scarcely possible that in a work like this we should be able to convey to the common reader a full knowledge of the methods of scientists in reaching their conclusions from spectrum analysis.

The spectrum presents to our eye a ray of light divided by refraction into seven clearly defined divisions, and each division or section is defined by its characteristic color. The order of division and colors always remaining the same. These colors are red, orange, yellow, green, blue, indigo and violet.

This spectrum of colors is produced by light rays moving in straight lines, each order of lines possessed of a distinct material structure. The red rays are called the heating rays, the green and yellow the illuminating rays, and the blue, indigo and violet the chemical or atomic rays. Accompanying this visible spectrum there are invisible rays of greater heating and chemical power than the visible, so that the heat is more intense below the red rays, and the chemical effects are greater above the violet.

Thus we have in light, *matter* drawn out in infinitely fine vibratory lines, and yet lines of such strength that they pursue their track through space in perfect, independent lines of force. These lines also seem to possess within themselves the power of motion. Now the chemist has found that each substance in matter, when reduced to its dynamic state in flame or in light, has its peculiar color and its angles of reflection, so that its color and place upon the spectrum can be accurately determined. Thus, "salts of copper give a blue color; soda flame is yellow, while the flame of potassa is of a beautiful violet color." Between the poles of a powerful voltaic battery, zinc gives a blue color in strata or bands, antimony a lilac color, mercury a pale blue, cadmium an intense green, arsenic a magnificent lilac, and bismuth a variety of colors undergoing rapid changes. The all-important fact that we wish to fix in the mind by thus bringing matter into a state of illumination is, that it in all cases is resolved into a force and at once assumes a linear order of motion. The metals are no exception to the law. "A flame containing several metals gives, at one and the same time, the characteristic bands of all." Another important fact must be noted that is to us more difficult of solution. If light from other sources pass through these metallic flames, like that from an electric lamp, they occasion dark bands in the spectrum precisely corresponding to the colored bands of their own emission.

The theory of our scientists is, that the flame of the metals absorbs or quenches their like, leaving a shadow instead of their appropriate color. In the solar spectrum these dark lines appear, and it is assumed that in the atmosphere of the sun the flames of these metals are crossed by the great volume of the sun's light, and these lines are cut out of the spectrum by such flames or vapors of incandescence. As the writer has no idea of matter being in an incandescent state in the sun, and especially the metals, he must discard the theory, while accepting the facts of metallic lines being detected in the spectrum of the sun and other heavenly bodies, as of the first importance. The dark lines belonging to iron, calcium, magnesium, sodium, chromium, etc., are found in the solar spectrum. These metals as a consequence are inferred to be constituents of the solar atmosphere.

That there is a determinate character given to the spectrum by the condition of the sun's electro-sphere cannot be doubted as it presents a different appearance when taken from different parts of the sun's surface. "The spots," says Prof. Proctor, "have not the same spectrum as the bright disc; the ordinarily bright parts have not the same spectrum as the exceptionally bright parts called the faculæ. Then the spectrum of the solar spots is variable, actually changing under the eye of the observer." We are then justified in clinging firmly to the theory that solar lines of light in the sun and on the earth responsively influence each other as the electro-magnetic lines of gravity influence each other between sun and earth. The sun and earth as two grand batteries and magnets furnishing the electrical strength by which the exchange of light and power is made. We love to think of these lines of light as the nerve cords of the solar system and as conveyers of all creative and material energy throughout the system. The thought is already before us that electrical currents also take up and carry matter in their passage through matter and that they also deposit matter when they meet with great resistance. This is just what we understand the electrical currents of light do at both sun and earth. They pass through space without resistance, but in the atmosphere of both sun and earth they encounter strong resistance, and as light is thereby evolved they both give off and receive material substances in a dynamic condition. It should be borne in mind that currents moving in the same direction attract each other, while those moving in opposite directions repel, consequently with equal attractions and repulsions these lines of light sweep the heavens from sun to earth and from earth to sun without interference, gathering up their oppositely charged currents of matter in their passage, and are always laden with the elements of material structures.

All that we desire, to place our hypothesis upon the solid basis of demonstration, rests in the accepted analysis of the solar spectrum, namely, that all of the primary elements in matter may be absorbed or taken up in the sunbeams, or, in more appropriate terms, in all forms of light in all worlds.

The grand office of light is thus disclosed to be the conveyance of matter to our earth as a builder, and this conveyance is made across the great distance separating earth from sun ; and not only this, it does the same work to a degree between stars and earth, for in star-light the presence of metallic substances is detected ; the conclusion is natural and we think inevitable that all world-building is by means of the light as a builder, and that it builds from itself. The hypothesis that it builds from sun to earth and planets and hence is a conveyer of a constant out-going energy from the sun without any return, is not consistent with Nature's great law, equivalents. Neither is it consistent to suppose that its work is simply a transfer of equal energy from sun to planets and from planets to sun, for in such a work there would be no world building. On our earth we find the work of upbuilding constantly going on. The earth has its marked periods of growth or of creative development. It in no respect can give back all it receives, and why may we not conclude that it is thus with both sun and planets? and if so, the grand work of building upon all of the bodies of the solar system must come in upon them from the moving forces of space, as we have before stated, and the light, laden with matter, we know is the builder.

In referring to the "sun as the source of power," Prof. Steele in his text-book on chemistry, says, "The sun warms, enlivens and animates the earth. In the laboratory of the leaf he produces the most wonderful chemical changes. We see his handiwork in the building of the forest, the carpeting of the meadow and the tinting of the rose. On the ladder of the sunbeam water climbs to the sky and falls again as rain. The very thunder of Niagara is but the sudden unbending of the spring that was first coiled by the sun in the evaporation from the ocean. **Up to the sun, then, we trace all the hidden manifestations of power.** Yet the force that produces such intricate and wide-extended changes is one twenty-three hundred millionth part of the tide that flows in every direction from this great central orb."

That such an energy as is here referred to comes in upon the earth through the influence of the sunlight there can be no doubt, but that the sun is the source of such energy increased by the difference between a globe 8,000 miles in diameter and the entire globe of the sun's influence, amounting to nearly six thousand millions of miles in diameter is a statement that is in direct opposition to the great law of gravity.

[NOTE. The comparison here made between the diameter of the solid body of the earth and the diameter of the sun's influence in the solar system does not seem just but it conforms to the theory of the schools, that the sun is the source of creative energy on the planets.]

By this law action and reaction are equal between all the heavenly bodies. According to this law the sun can give only as he receives. Like any other organized body of matter he must receive strength from some source equal to the amount of work he is constantly performing. He can only build his sunbeams into the planets as he is built upon by the energy that comes in upon him from the mighty attractions that extend from the sun to the outermost planet of the solar system.

The same light and energy that come to our earth as building and controlling forces are the same in the sun from whence they come. Hence, instead of regarding the sun as a great waster we should regard him as a great gatherer. He is a great giver because he is strengthened by a vast globe of forces extending around him to the distance of three thousand millions of miles. All that he expends of his munificent strength is the comparatively small measure that the planets receive, and the outermost planets as we have seen shine by their own light and as sun systems impart of their strength at the command of the sun's attracting energy. The hypothesis we present regards the whole solar system as consisting of a vast globe of electrical forces weighted with the elements of matter as the spectrum has revealed in the sunlight, and that with an unfailing energy they are building from without upon the sun and planetary bodies of the system, and that this process of building has been carried forward from the beginning of all aggregations of matter as evolutions from the dynamic energy of space.

We thus reach that unity from the facts of Nature, after which all scientific thought is now searching, and we have merely followed the guiding star of demonstrable scientific truths.

CHAPTER XXIV.

SUN AND PLANETS. ARE THEY INHABITED?

IN calculating the power of magnets, two conditions of power must be considered: 1, The magnitude of the magnetic body, and 2, The number and length of the electrical currents that encircle the magnet. In constructing instruments of great electrical power, systems of several wires, thoroughly insulated, are so arranged that according to the principle of induction, broken currents acting and reacting upon each other by means of rapidly uniting and breaking circuits, serve to multiply power.

You have doubtless already fixed in your minds the fact that the soft iron core of the horse-shoe magnet is endowed with its strength from induced currents of magnetism, coming in upon it under the command of the electrical current passed around it in its coiled envelope of insulated wire. The passing current is not allowed the least possible electrical connection with the encircled iron core, and yet it becomes saturated with induced magnetic currents of great strength.

On the other hand, were the core of the magnet made of steel instead of iron and thoroughly magnetized, so as to become a permanent magnet, the magnetism of the permanent magnet would cause induced electrical currents to pass in the wires around it. So by bringing a wire traversed by an electrical current suddenly near to another wire in its natural state, a current of electricity will instantaneously be developed in the latter wire, or if suddenly removed from it a current would also pass in the natural wire. Hence, by uniting and breaking the current of the charged wire, an induced current would be made to pass back and forth through the natural wire, its rapidity governed by the opening and closing of the circuit of the electrical current in the battery wire. "Thus, by a simple mechanical action, making an electrified wire or a magnet move in close proximity to a natural wire, an induced current was produced in the natural wire of very short duration, but capable of becoming increasingly energetic, according to the rapidity of the motion of the electrified wire," and by this discovery of electrical and magnetic induction made by Faraday, the grand results of advancing electrical science, for the last half century have been attained, and yet there has been among our best scientists a lack of clear conceptions respecting the distinction to be noted as existing in Nature, between electricity and magnetism. Ampere regarded magnets and currents as identical, and taught that "magnets are bodies traversed continually by electric currents."

Baile, a French scientist, says, "Here are two series of facts, magnetic phenomena and electric phenomena, separated to this day, yet coming together and confounding themselves with one another," and he seems to adopt the thought of Ampere, that "one and the same cause may produce effects differing from one another."

Now, it seems to us, that while magnetic and electrical currents induce each other, and may be converted into each other, that there is this marked and all-important difference between them. Electricity moves in unbroken currents through space, having its home in space, while magnetism moves in broken and polarized currents through body, bound to a magnetic center, thus having its home in body. This distinction we have already made, but we need to review the thought here, as our hypothesis is based upon the belief that all of creation is under the guidance of these two great correlate forces, and that all of space is endowed with electrical orbital currents, crossed by radial magnetic currents, and in the rapid and natural interchange of these currents of space with the currents of body, all the mechanical evolutions of creation are secured. It is clearly evident that the great principle of induction is the pivotal center between electrical and magnetic phenomena. They work over against each other across the dividing line between body and space. Magnetic bodies treasure up power, and are constantly strengthened by the work they perform. This treasured power or unfailing strength of the magnet, is an induced power, derived from the inducing currents of electricity that circulate around it, so that the electrical currents of space are the nursing currents of magnetized bodies. All organizations of matter are perfected under the nursing forces of electrical circles that play around all magnetic bodies, and impart perennial strength to all of the building forces that permeate them. It is but a step from the contemplation of this principle of magnetic strength treasured up in the magnet, constantly fed from the inducing currents of space, to the contemplation of the sun, as the great reservoir of magnetic strength equal to the task of driving the entire machinery of the solar system. I grant this is a thought that almost overpowers the imagination. It seems almost profane to attempt such a survey of the grand display of creative power as appears in the heavens, but an open door is here set before us into the outer courts of the great temple reared as by divine command, where we can view as sons of God, the work that has been carried forward during the ages, without the sound of a hammer or the confused jargon of the workmen; and shall we not enter? There surely can only be a blessing in the search after the hidden builders of Nature's grand temples.

In the mechanism of creation there is a self-working energy in constant play between elements and development that brings under tribute both matter and force. There is a unity of result and perfection of structure secured by the interworking and harmonious combination of the elements of matter marshaled under the direction of living and self-guiding forces.

Both matter and energy have a part to play, a work to perform, and are constantly fulfilling their mission as builders. Out of themselves come forth wonderful creations, as births spring from living parentage, multiplying and developing in their order all of the possibilities of life and being, of power and structure. From the natural and possibly divinely established union between force and matter, as between power and machine, the work of creation moves forward. The power always in supply and the machine always responding to its touch.

The rhythm of force currents moving through our own

bodies, going forth from brain and heart, perpetuating our being, is but the hum of the machinery that is working in all of the various orders of being that inhabit all worlds, so that worlds in their order are built up, sustained and guided by force currents that move through them, constituting them machines as well as bodies; hence, in contemplating the formation of our system of worlds we are compelled to regard them as living wheels of a grand system of machinery that is moved by the force currents of creative power. There is a machine structure to all of Nature's works set up for the application of working power and a power is ever present to take possession of all rising structures. With this view of creation it follows that we are to regard sun and planets as great reservoirs of working forces adequate to the supply of the great energy that holds them in place and gives them their wonderful velocities of daily and annual revolution.

Let us endeavor to gain full possession of the thought here passing before us. If we could but take our places with the favored dwellers in the sun and could there gain adequate conceptions of the sun's magnitude and power, we would drop out of our creeds the thought of our race of human beings standing at the head of created intelligences. We should cease to regard this grand system of worlds only made for man, and even the great sun himself created simply to furnish light for our dwellings and warmth and nourishment for our bodies.

We would there find a globe of vast magnitude revolving in a constantly illuminated atmosphere.

The light of the stars would be quenched, and the light

that would seem to come from other bodies would seem so insignificant that the thoughts of a self-luminous atmosphere would take possession of the mind. Great shadows, high mountains and deep valleys doubtless break up the sun's day, so that in his own surroundings there are provisions for that diversity of landscape and climate that are needful for the highest orders of mind.

The tropical regions of South America present a structural arrangement of mountains, valleys and high plains, of such a nature as to furnish all varieties of climate that may be desired under the most powerful rays of a tropical sun, teaching us that the surface structure of a planet may be made a compensation for change of seasons and temperature arising from revolution of the earth.

The immense size of the sun's body affords ample scope for the variety of structure needed. It furnishes material for the largest display and grandest variety of surface changes suited to climatic modifications such as appear under the equator upon the earth.

Again, the light of the sun is distributed over the entire body of the sun with increased intensity under the disturbing influence of the eight planets that reciprocally give their light to each other; also the poles of the sun are at a vast distance from central points of illumination under the planets on his equator.

The great spots that are seen upon the sun tell us plainly that there are mountains of observation thrusting themselves up through the sun's photosphere, from which his inhabitants may gain a knowledge of outlying worlds. Be this as it may, we are compelled to regard the sun as both the great illuminator of the solar system, and the grand reservoir of all his creative and moving forces, and it would seem to us like reversing the order of Nature that he should dispense benefits that are not native in the elements of his own organization; or that he should cause a profusion of life to spring up on one and we believe all of the planets of the solar system, and not have a grander profusion of being springing forth from his own body. All of the conditions of life, and life of a high order, are found in the elements of the sun's organism, and we can but regard it as a matter of necessity, that the highest and most perfect orders of being should appear there.

If life in the sun follow the orders of evolutionary development as seen upon the earth, it must have secured orders of intellectual beings for transcending those of man, and yet beings of material form.

In the sun there has been gathered a vast body of matter under the constant influence of solar light, and subject to the constant play of magnetic forces.

These furnish the grand conditions of life and growth, and in fact magnetization, and organization of body and development of life, invariably follow each other in their order upon the earth, and why not in the sun?

The reasons for regarding the sun as more highly magnetic than the planets are,

1. His power is sufficient to make him the balancing center of all the planets and satellites and to control them in their orbits. This is demonstrative of vast magnetic strength.

2. His illuminating energy is greatly superior in inten-

sity to that of the planets, and we have seen from these papers that such illumination is caused by the action and reaction of electro-magnetic currents of force between sun and planets. The principle of induction also teaches, as the circle of electrical currents that play around the sun extend out from him at a working distance of twenty-six hundred millions of miles, it must possess within its organic structure a system of magnetic currents of equal strength as a balance of energy. Another cause of increased magnetic strength is his rapid revolution in the face of the incoming attractions from the planetary bodies.

The sun revolves at the rate of some 4,000 miles per hour, and at eight points in his circuit of revolution the planets pour in upon him disturbing attractions. These eight tides of forces come to the sun's body as retarding forces that must be overcome by the revolving strength of his internal magnetic forces which are strengthened by the burden of the work thus done. A rapid making and breaking magnetic currents always multiplies power. The rapid pulsations of magnetic currents from equator to poles of the sun that are disturbed and broken by planetary currents must fill the body with a flow of magnetic strength of immense magnitude, such as the great light of his body reveals.

Comparing the sun with our earth we find his diameter some 110 times greater,—that while we can visit the regions of our north pole by a journey of less than 6,000 miles from the equator, that if an inhabitant of the sun it would require a journey of 660,000 miles, and then that while large tracts of country lying around our north and south poles are locked in the cold embrace of perpetual winter, the entire body of the sun is surrounded by a constantly luminous atmosphere, and that the long lines of magnetic energy that are made to play so rapidly through his body from equator to poles serve as warming and stimulating agencies to secure the production of every species of life under the most favorable conditions of development.

With this view of the immense organism of the sun, and with the principles of illumination as presented in these papers, we gain the grandest conceptions possible of the conditions of life in the broad expanse of the sun's fields of perennial verdure, and its groves and forests of unbounded extent and magnificent grandeur, and upon its oceans, seas, lakes and rivers that outrival our highest conceptions of majesty and beauty. We have been told of a land where there should be no need of the sun, or of the moon to enlighten it, and that there was no night there and we have still failed to gain any conception of such a land as fashioned from material creations, and yet such a world the sun is, and we doubt not inhabited with high orders of being that pass through stages and conditions of life similar to our own.

As the sun is the balancing body of the solar system and holds all the forces of the system under the control of his commanding energy, it is but reasonable to conclude that in the distribution of orders of life, he should be more highly endowed than all of the planetary worlds taken in the aggregate.

The importance of the sun in the solar system has been

heretofore estimated from its beneficent work of dispensing light and heat to the planets; it has consequently been regarded as a vast generating furnace of consuming combustible matter, from which light and heat have been radiated for millions of years, throughout the entire field of planetary motion.

Various have been the theories concerning its sources of supply of combustible matter, as we have already seen. Nebulous masses have been supposed to have poured their half-formed bodies into it, across the orbits of the planets. Gravitation has been supposed to have gone counter to all laws of gravity, and to have driven such bodies in right lines of motion toward the sun's body and thus generated inconceivable masses of gravital flame. Again it has been supposed that a vast residuary mass of heat was treasured up in the sun at that time when burning worlds were thrown off from his molten body amid a grand nebulous conflagration, and that while all of these bodies have lost their nebulous flame and parted with their radial heat, yet the parent sun has retained a supply from which they have been drawing for all the purposes of life and motion for millions of years, and still gives no evidences of exhaustion.

With these hypotheses filling our text-books of science, and repeated in the literature of the past, it is not strange that the sun has been regarded of but little more account to the solar system than the cooking stoves in our kitchens or the coal grates of our fire-places to the social life of the household. Thus the grand old king of day has been degraded to a servant while he has been a ruler. He has been but little thought of as a nourisher of the teeming orders of life within his own radiant fields of vast capabilities and unmeasured boundaries, while he has constantly marshaled all the elements of life, and caused to spring forth from matter all of the supplies needed for the nourishment and sustenance of all forms of being in both earth and planets.

He has been supposed to give to earth and planets every thing that makes life possible, while he has been consuming his own strength. He has been regarded as gleaning the gathering elements of matter from space into his own burning bosom that he may send forth from his raging furnaces of destruction the beneficence of the sunbeam, to become a nourisher of life and a builder of all living organisms in the family of the planets. It is a wonder to us that against such misconceptions of creative wisdom human thought has not long since revolted. It does not seem wise that a globe of 850,000 miles in diameter should be doomed to ages of wasting, and finally to utter extinction simply to make habitable a body like our earth, of only 8,000 miles in diameter, and perchance one or more other planets.

Before proceeding further with our inquiries respecting the probable inhabitable condition of sun and planets, we ought to note carefully the conditions under which life is developed. Leaving out of mind all controversial questions respecting the origin of species, we find that light, heat and moisture are the leading elements of force in the production of the various orders of life. The elements of the atmosphere we find, wherever these forms are in active play, as they are in the combinations of the atmosphere, the carrying and distributing agencies of light, heat and moisture. In the Mosaic account of creation, light and the waters came together, before vegetable life appeared. We have regarded light as illuminated currents of gravity coming from the mutual attractions of sun and earth, and broken up into polarized atoms by the magnetic currents of the earth. Moisture, we well know, is a necessary agent in distributing or diffusing electricity, and it is alike necessary to distribute the light. Thus we find a warm humid atmosphere favorable to life growths. In such an atmosphere there is a highly magnetized condition of all forms within it. In such an atmosphere currents of electricity cannot easily be gathered and retained upon the prime conductor of the electrical machine. The reason for this is, that light and heat are preparing to enter into material combinations by means of the magnetization of earth currents. This leads us to affirm that magnetization or polarization of light is necessary to the development of life, and that we have a right to expect life upon the surface of the planets wherever there exists a highly magnetized atmosphere.

The planet's relative position as to nearness to the sun has therefore but little effect upon the question of its adaptation to the conditions of either animal or plant life.

In the torrid zone there is snow on the upper slopes of lofty mountains during the whole year, while at the base of these mountains there may be the luxuriance of tropical life.

Our scientists tell us that this is because of the rare atmosphere of the mountain tops, while they do not tell us why it is so rare when it is thousands of feet nearer the sun than the atmosphere of the valleys.

Our reason for such a fact, is, that the strength of the magnetic currents on the tops of mountains is not sufficient to break up the direct sun currents or direct rays of the sun's light, and hence there is no polarization and diffusion of light, and hence a light and highly electrical atmosphere with the thin rays of the sun unbroken by polarization or magnetization, and hence, the cold atmosphere of the mountains.

By consulting our astronomical charts, we shall find that the light and heat of the planets are calculated with reference to the distance they are from the sun, and yet the tops of the mountains teach us that as we ascend towards the sun we reach into regions of eternal frost. In an article from the pen of Richard A. Proctor in St. Nicholas we find him saying, "That Venus, beautiful though she looks, would not be a comfortable home for us. In the first place, we know that if we draw nearer to a fire we get more heat from it. Now Venus is much nearer the sun—the great fire of the solar system—than our earth is. She receives then much more heat from him. In fact, it is easily calculated that if our earth were set traveling on the path of Venus, we should receive almost exactly twice as much heat from the sun as we do at present. This would be unbearable, except, perhaps, in the polar regions; and even there the summer with the sun above the horizon all through the twenty-four hours, would be scarcely bearable. Besides what a contrast between the hot polar summer and the cold polar winter, when for weeks together the sun would not be seen at all. Altogether, this earth would be a miserable home for us if her path were as close to the sun as that of Venus."

According to this method of reasoning Venus has a very uncomfortable position in relation to the heat of the sun and yet between Venus and the sun there is the intense and perpetual cold of stellar space.

The truth is, nearness to the sun has nothing whatever to do with the evolution of light or heat upon the planets. As light and heat are evolved just where there is inflammable matter to supply them with light and heat energy, so the light and heat energy of the planets are the reservoirs of energy that determine their supplies of warmth and illumination.

In the outermost planets of the solar system, there are evidences of self-enlightening, inferior sun systems, with revolving satellites to supply any light and heat they might lack by means of distance from the sun. The position we assume is this: That wherever magnetization is carried forward in matter, there Nature is rearing her structures, and wherever these forces build worlds they also promote organization, they give life ; and wherever the lower organizations of life begin, the crowning results are the higher orders of being. In the building of the earth Nature has drawn largely upon the organizing forces of living creatures.

Our chalk cliffs and ocean beds, and coral reefs and islands, our rock structures of coal and lime, our alluvial deposits, all tell us that the forces of life go hand in hand with the forces of earth creation. Every atom of matter that goes to its place in organization goes under the charge of the same forces that give life. In fact, creation draws upon life forces to perfect and guide in the formation of all of its varied structures. As the bird builds its nest for the young life that is to be nurtured within it, so all of Nature's work in rearing earth-structures is for the varied forms of life that shall crown them with a completeness, revealing harmony and wisdom. With these views of the relation of life to structural organisms, we say that sun and planets are not only adapted to the higher orders of life, but that nothing short of a miracle can keep them from being inhabited.

According to what we see of creation upon the earth, it is no miracle to create species and establish orders of being, but rather a miracle to prevent creation.

As to atmosphere, clouds, moisture, rivers, seas and oceans, we know there must be atmosphere where there is light, and light and gravity being the same forces, and all forms of creation being evolved from these forces, it follows that all worlds constitute a single unity of being, and having such unity, they are fashioned under the same laws of forces and must be after the same likeness.

CHAPTER XXV.

ETERNAL FORCES: MIND AND MATTER.

IN our investigations of electro-magnetic forces we have found them to be closely allied to matter. There is a materiality about them that submits to material tests. We measure the length of the polarized atoms of the sunbeam. We can multiply and divide the strength of magnetic currents. We can calculate the strength and velocity with which they move through body, and weigh their influence over organized masses of matter, and yet they are so ethereal in character that they seem to belong to a spiritual order of existence, to an order of creation vastly superior to our world of tangible and sensitive forms of being. But in carefully noting the wonders of these forms we find them always under command, subject to exact laws of control. They attract and repel, select and reject, move through body and through space, lift atoms, warm, enlighten and control worlds, and yet in no case do they manifest intelligence in selection or will power in the execution of their grand displays of power. There is not a change takes place in body or a development in organization, or an order of life in our world, but is subject to the control of electrical and magnetic forces, and yet in all changes, in all growths, in all orders of creation there is not the deviation of an atom or an influence from the laws of electrical order and control that indicates the presence of thought or the perceptions of reason.

The sunlight always moves in the same lines of order and always bears with it the same elements of strength and is constantly performing the same work. Magnetic and electrical attractions and repulsions, though they move with the velocity of light and weigh all matter as in scales and take charge of all atoms, conveying each to its true place in body, yet never vary from the exact measure of mathematical law. Their balance of matter is exact to the weight of an atom, and the inverse order of the squares of distances is always the limit of their influence.

In the mechanism of creation, under the charge of these forces there is a perfection of order and a constancy of motion that the progress of the ages cannot change. But to study the nature of these forces and the order of their work we have been led into realms of pure thought, in which visions of creative strength become trusty guides, and where we find networks of living lines of strength, that, though unseen by the natural eye, preside over all of the rising structures of material development.

By tracing out the lines of attraction of that unseen power which our philosophers have named gravity, and by classifying the phenomena of its intercommunion with all forms of matter, and its guidance of all planetary motion, we have found that the foundations of all material structures are laid upon the unseen elements of space, that move with the velocity of lightning and with the strength of omnipotence. We have been slow to recognize the presence of these strong and living lines of space because we have thought there was nothing material except that which can be distinguished by the contact of the senses.

The sub-sensible world we have called spiritual, and those displays of power that lie beyond the cognizance of the senses we have classed under the works of a purely spiritual being whom we have called God. Thus we have separated the spiritual from the material by the cold, dark mysteries of the great depths that surround matter. In our imagination we have regarded God and spirits as dwelling apart at an infinite remove from man and matter, heaven no where and man and matter from no whence. God eternal, matter an accident, and man and all orders of life mere creatures of a spiritual mechanism. We have been exceedingly jealous of any efforts on the part of human reason to clear away the mysterious depths that seem to separate so widely the purely spiritual from the grossly material. Hence we have been taught that matter is cold and dead, that its only province in the mechanism of worlds is to be acted upon, and its only exercise of power consisted in the dead weight of inertia. All else we have ascribed to God and a mysterious agency that we have called the law of gravity, and thus we have resolved all force into gravity and God, both unseen and unknown, and dwelling apart from each other so far as correlation of existence is concerned.

With this bald materialism on one hand and sublimated spiritualism on the other, it has been like the efforts of the Son of God to walk upon the waters of the lake of Genneserat, for our men of science to trust their convictions of truth and follow where their increasing insight, by way of experiment into the heretofore hidden secrets of material creative potency, would lead.

That faith, which is commended as so sublime a virtue in religious dogma, is regarded with suspicion, and classed as infidel and presumptuous on the part of the worshipers of God through the revelations of divinity, in the works of creation.

In these papers we have dared to go wherever the advancing light of the illuminated cloud of creative forces has led, and we have found material forces more potent than matter, stronger and firmer, and more enduring than any conceptions of material foundations of worlds upon which our spiritualistic philosophers have endeavored to build. We have seen that under the sensitive touch of these forces, all organisms of matter are filled with the life currents of creation, and that matter, so far from being cold and dead, is warmed with the constant play of life-forces around it, and within it, touching each atom with a commanding and warming energy. We have also found that what we have heretofore regarded as void space, is the grand treasury of Nature's creative elements of life and strength; and that from these the work of all the grand industries of creation is promoted, building up all organizations of matter, promoting all growths and evolving in their order all forms and conditions of life. In the work that is done by revolving the great magnets of sun and planets, it is easy to trace the wonderful presence of these constantly moving forces; but this displays simply the most palpable exercise of power, not the most wonderful and sensitively creative. The work that evolves sunlight from the broken electrical currents upon the surface of the planets—that carries this light to every living thing upon all globes—that builds itself into every form of evolving matter and every form of life-growth on land and in the waters—that carries forward the circulation of all fluids in living bodies, and through earth structures—that warms with a generous flow of stimulating energy the secret fountains of life in all living bodies—that waits upon every atom of matter, whether moving in space, incorporated into body, or passing through the transformations of growths, and determines the order of their motion, that presides over the secret forces that produce chemical changes in the earth, that warms with rapidly passing currents all rolling worlds from center to circumference, from equator to poles with an energy that promotes organic life, presides over crystallization and converts the evolving gases into the solid structures that rest in the deep foundations of the mountains, is the work that the forces of gravity are constantly performing, and they rest not, night or day. They never grow weary, always hastening to complete their circuit of power without wasting of strength or the loss of the smallest fraction of a second of time.

In this long catalogue of the work of electrical and magnetic forces through the great magnets of sun, planets and satellites, we have purposed to compass the order and the methods of creative energy in all worlds, and yet we do not for a moment cherish the thought that by unfolding this order of creative work under the control of the material forces that fill immensity, that there is, therefore, no great creative mind that is God over all. The perfection of creative energy in material structures reaches out after the higher and nobler forces of spiritual being. The fact that we can take up the story of creation and read it backward to its beginning of order, that we can catechise the forces and listen to the hum of their industries and number the advancing steps of their progress, is a revelation of something superior to matter, of an agency that presides over creative forces, that thinks, reasons, and even commands material potencies.

This supreme agency, involving memory, perception, thought, reflection, reason, and presiding over all *will*, or mental potentiality, is as truly a factor in the great world problem as the material forces that we have studied with so much interest.

This agency has its place in the problem, not simply as an idea, as a conception, but as a force. It is a force that is self-asserting, self-determining and self-guiding. It is not, like the potentiality of matter, always governed by an evenly poised balance. If the human will were always conditioned by a commanding energy, either of intellectuality or of materiality, it could be canceled from the problem, but the sentiment of the world holds the human will responsible for its exercise of power, and from its decisions gains conceptions of justice and injustice, of wisdom and folly, of truth and error.

This lifts the mind forces of man that we denominate soul to a plane superior to that of material forces. The human will can antagonize and condition matter and by so doing it reveals its kingship. It is necessary that we acquaint ourselves with the will as a force superior to material forces before we can acquaint ourselves with God as a Creator. In the view we have taken of material forces we have to admit that the argument of the theist, that professes to demonstrate the existence and character of God from the evidence of design and perfection of order in creation, is greatly weakened, if not destroyed, but by so doing we elevate and ennoble spiritual forces. As we have already stated, it is the province of mind to command, and it is also the province of material energy to obey, and we here add that material obedience is a perfect obedience and a constant obedience. Nature's methods of work are forever the same, save as there be an ascending series from the small to the great, from the simple to the complex, from the germ of the beginning to the completed realization of the possible. In such perfection of order, and with such potency of energy as we find in creation's works we can see no more call for a Deity to originate species than to perpetuate them.

We can conceive of Deity as commanding the hosts of heaven in their order, of ordering the progressions of life and being upon the earth, but we cannot conceive Deity creating material things independent of material forces.

And then we cannot think of Deity as setting apart a day, a week, or an age to the creation of species, as a special work reserved to Himself, and then passing these patterns over to material forces to copy, age after age. Nay verily, so far as creative forces are concerned there is a constant and progressive order of beginnings in all forms of life, as truly as a constant order of reproduction.

In reaching our conceptions of material forces, we first gained a knowledge of their presence in matter as displayed in the battery and in the magnet. We found these forces subtle, refined, all-pervading and omnipotent. We found them sovereigns over matter, and having a life-potency prior to all aggregations of matter. By a like order of reasoning would we seek after a true conception of mind-force and press the thought up to the conception of God as the crowning excellency of all life, and all orders of being.

We find that the best temples of creative work on our earth are for the human soul to dwell in, and there is but a single step to the conception, that the crowning glory of creation's universal work, is, to prepare palaces for the dwelling places of a sublime order of thinking, reasoning, immortal beings. When we learn that the material forces moving in space unseen, constitute a network of strength that holds all worlds to their paths of light and order, we shall be prepared to think of spiritual forces that are real, and that hold within their orders of work, all possibilities of creative mind forces for all ranks of immortal spirits. As we have found all creative work on our planet, and all material growths clothed with the shining drapery of the light, we can take in the conception of the dwelling place of spirits as a dwelling place of sublime perfection and beauty. But we have anticipated our argument hoping thereby to prepare our minds for pursuing it with more trust and clearer convictions than we might otherwise gain.

We find in the electro-magnet as constructed by Prof.

Henry, that by uniting the surrounding wire with the galvanic battery it was instantly endowed with a power capable of lifting more than two thousand pounds. Our conclusion is, that a real, unseen presence passed through the wires of the battery, whose strength was a fixed determinate reality; having weight of 2,056 pounds.

From this real presence of an unseen force, gathered from space with the rapidity of the lightning's flash, we built our argument respecting the dynamic energy that is in space sovereign over matter.

But Prof. Henry had by careful thought and effort constructed the magnet so as to elicit such a power, and by bringing to his aid a fulcrum and lever, the Professor by the application of his own strength could lift the weight at will. In such an event will-power reveals an efficiency superior to material force, in that the one is reflective and self-moved, while the other is simply material energy. As we noted the strength of the magnet by the sum of 2,056 pounds, so we note the weight of thought-force in the mind of the Professor at the same number, and thus we balance material force with thought-force. We note a distinct difference between these agencies of power that marks the superiority of the one over the other, and with this distinction in mind we may affirm that the world of spirit and of thought is as truly a demonstrable fact as the world of matter and material force.

But the clear thinker comes to us with the thought that the human body is a battery and magnet of superior workmanship to that prepared by the skill of the Professor and that after all material force should take the first place.

We reply that in the comparison the one is clothed with the personality of thought, reason and will, and appears as an intelligent commander, while the other appears as a mere bundle of instruments nicely fashioned and adapted to work as a servant. Again, it may be urged, that the mind dwells in a structure of material workmanship, and without it the mind is an impossibility. We reply, that as the body is constituted the servant of the mind so it is its office to prepare for the mind its palace and to bear it upon its shoulders as a royal guest. We may be questioned one step further and asked: If the soul hold an independent personality, separate from the brain structure, at what point of the dual being is the union joined?

We answer at the sensitive touch of that magnetic force that is the most refined and subtle energy of body, and which is ordained as the communing force between life and body, between mind and material energy.

At such a point of union between the spiritual and material the soul touches the magnetic keys of brain, as the musician touches the keys of a well tuned instrument and thus gives voice to his thoughts of harmony.

Thus when we have pressed our thoughts of material forces up to the vanishing line of materiality, to a magnetic sovereignty in matter, we find it there touches the boundaries of spiritual forces and of spiritual personalities, that are as real and as self-affirming as the forces and agencies of matter.

We are thus enabled to pass the open door of pure reason, to a world of spiritual agencies that holds its rank above and superior to our world of matter and of material forces. But are we here confronted with the religious sceptic, who has materialized both God and heaven, and asked, "How can these things be?" we return the answer, "That which is born of spirit is spirit." What that personality in us, is, which we affirm in our struggles after possession, ownership, and the comforts and pleasures of life, we cannot tell in the language of material symbols. We can give to it no measure, we can not gain a conception of it that can be sketched by pen or pencil. It has in us an ideal personality. It asserts its presence as a power by its acts of power, but it always hides its presence, as the world of pure spirits is hid from our view. Let no one turn from this struggle of mind to gain possession of thought-images that can only hold a place in the realms of pure reason, baffled and disheartened, to solace the mind with the tangible things of matter, as some Baal worshipers cling to their religious creeds, saying "these are realities and are teachers of truths beyond which we do not care to go." They will find in the mathematical measurements of body and space, problems equally perplexing to our thoughts of spirit and of a spiritual world.

The solar system appears to us, in lines of material measurement, utterly incomprehensible.

The distance of our earth from the sun is set down at some 90,000,000 of miles, a number out-reaching human thought, as a measure. Then Neptune has a distance from the sun thirty times greater than that of the earth. Let the materialist struggle to gain an idea of the boundaries of the solar system and he is lost in his reckoning; and if lost here, how can he grapple with the thoughts of the Universe, measured by his own dear standards that are fixed material measures?

But we have found that even matter ignores such standards of measure. Material forces themselves prefer to measure distances by heart throbs rather than by millions of miles. The earth and sun hold a magnetic communion with each other, so as to exchange greetings in lines of light in every eight minutes of time, and the magnetic strength of the sun pulsates from center to circumference of the solar system, in only four hours of time. Thus by the standard of that ethereal essence that separates the spiritual world from the material, creation is brought within the grasp of human thought, and a conception of a world of spiritual reality gains a lodgment in the pure conceptions of even human reason. This sympathetic union is preserved under the constant flow of the sunlight and planet-light, across the vast intervals that separate suns and planets.

It would here afford us great pleasure to call attention to the abundant evidence that we have of the sensitive and apparently nervous system of forces that extends throughout the solar system; but the plan of our work forbids anything like an exhaustive treatment of the subjects brought under our general theme. It is sufficient for us to state that the magnetic currents of the earth, that are detected by the vibrations of the magnetic needle, and the system of suspended magnets used in the United States coast survey at their posts of observation, are always responsive to apparent magnetic changes upon the surface of the sun. The changed polarity between earth and sun occasioned by the daily revolution of the earth, arising from the earth's inclination to the plane of her orbit, causes daily corresponding vibrations of the magnetic needle. These changes are 15' in summer and 10' in winter. From about 8 A. M. to 1 P. M. the north pole moves to the west and swings slowly back until 10 P. M. It then moves west until 3 A. M., returning to its starting point at 8 A. M. The careful observation of these magnetic changes that arise from temporary disturbances of the sun's photosphere, is the basis upon which rest the weather prophecies of climatic changes upon the earth. The sun-spots always indicate their presence by their disturbance of these magnetic currents of the earth.

These facts of matter, and these seemingly solid structures of planets, with their foundations of granite and their vast measures of oceans and seas, mountains and plains, yield a perfect obedience to a subtle magnetic agency that at best, marks but an insensible line between a world of matter and a world of spirits. The majesty of matter here bows to that wonderful potency that gathers the grand potencies of the solar system in a single grasp, and touches every atom of matter and compasses its entire circuits of motion in a period of time of insignificant measure.

But a step beyond such an essence and such a potency the mind needs to go to think of God and spirits, to think of mind forces and mind measures that make a spirit-world their dwelling place, and earth and matter their footstool.

CONTENTS.

CHAPTER I.
Laws and Modes of Motion.................. 9–19

CHAPTER II.
First Things........................... 20–48

CHAPTER III.
The Mysteries of the Magnet............... 49–60

CHAPTER IV.
Gravitation............................ 61–67

CHAPTER V.
Gravitation and Planetary Motion.......... 68–85

CHAPTER VI.
Evolution of Light...................... 86–93

CHAPTER VII.
Heat, Light and Life.................... 94–111

CHAPTER VIII.
Across the Border...................... 112–121

CHAPTER IX.
Fourth State of Matter.................. 122–124

CHAPTER X.
Unity of the Forces.................... 125–131

CHAPTER XI.
Nature's Methods in Creation 132–135

CHAPTER XII.
Attraction and Repulsion Equal Factors in Gravitation.................................. 136–143

CHAPTER XIII.
Sources of Light and Heat.......................... 144–156

CHAPTER XIV.
Light as a Builder................................. 157–165

CHAPTER XV.
Scientific Revelations............................. 166–180

CHAPTER XVI.
The Unseen World.................................. 181–186

CHAPTER XVII.
Latent and Sensible Power......................... 187–195

CHAPTER XVIII.
Radiant Matter and Mechanical Power............... 196–207

CHAPTER XIX.
From Whence Rocks................................. 208–214

CHAPTER XX.
Form and Motion of Planets Determine Their Origin.. 215–225

CHAPTER XXI.
Life and Radiant Matter........................... 226–228

CHAPTER XXII.
Evolution of Life................................. 229–246

CHAPTER XXIII.
Testimony of the Spectrum......................... 247–261

CHAPTER XXIV.
Sun and Planets. Are They Inhabited?.............. 262–276

CHAPTER XXV.
Eternal Forces: Mind and Matter................... 277–289

www.ingramcontent.com/pod-product-compliance
Lightning Source LLC
Chambersburg PA
CBHW031332230426
43670CB00006B/318